Mountain Biking Lake Tahoe

Help Us Keep This Guide Up to Date

Every effort has been made by the author and editors to make this guide as accurate and use-ful as possible. However, many things can change after a guide is published—trails are rerouted, regulations change, techniques evolve, facilities come under new management, etc.

We would love to hear from you concerning your experiences with this guide and how you feel it could be improved and kept up to date. While we may not be able to respond to all comments and suggestions, we'll take them to heart, and we'll also make certain to share them with the author. Please send your comments and suggestions to the following address:

The Globe Pequot Press
Reader Response/Editorial Department
P.O. Box 480
Guilford, CT 06437

Or you may e-mail us at:

editorial@GlobePequot.com

Thanks for your input, and happy trails!

Mountain Biking
Lake Tahoe

A Guide to Lake Tahoe and Truckee's Greatest Off-Road Bicycle Rides

Lorene Jackson

FALCON GUIDES®

GUILFORD, CONNECTICUT
HELENA, MONTANA
AN IMPRINT OF THE GLOBE PEQUOT PRESS

A **FALCON** GUIDE ®

Falcon, FalconGuide, and fat/trax are registered trademarks of Morris Book Publishing, LLC.

Text design by Nancy Freeborn
Maps created by XNR Productions Inc. © Morris Book Publishing, LLC
Spine photo by Daniel Bailey
Photos by Lorene Jackson

Library of Congress Cataloging-in-Publication Data
Jackson, Lorene.
  Mountain biking Lake Tahoe : a guide to Lake Tahoe and Truckee's greatest off-road bicycle rides / Lorene Jackson.– 1st ed.
       p. cm. – (A Falcon guide)
  Includes index.
  ISBN-13: 978-0-7627-2696-7
  ISBN-10: 0-7627-2696-2
  1. All terrain cycling–Tahoe, Lake (Calif. and Nev.)–Guidebooks. 2. All terrain cycling–Truckee (Calif.)–Guidebooks. 3. Tahoe, Lake (Calif. and Nev.)–Guidebooks. 4. Truckee (Calif.)–Guidebooks. I. Title. II. Series.
  GV1045.5.T34J33 2006
  917.94'380454–dc22

                                              2006001823

Manufactured in the United States of America
First Edition/Second Printing

To buy books in quantity for corporate use or incentives, call **(800) 962–0973** or e-mail **premiums@GlobePequot.com**.

The author and The Globe Pequot Press assume no liability for accidents happening to, or injuries sustained by, readers who engage in the activities described in this book.

To my family—every loving one of you.

Contents

Acknowledgments x
Get Ready to Crank! 1
    Welcome to Lake Tahoe 1
    Weather 2
    Altitude 2
    Flora and Fauna 3
    Wilderness Restrictions and Regulations 3
    IMBA Rules of the Trail 4
    How to Use This Book 5
    How to Use the Maps 5
    Go Forth 6
    Map Legend 7
    Ride Finder 8

Lake Tahoe 11
  1. General Creek Loop with Out-and-Back to Lost Lake 12
  2. Blackwood Canyon to Ellis Lake Out-and-Back 15
  3. Lower Blackwood Canyon Loop 19
  4. Stanford Rock Loop 22
  5. Page Meadows Double Loop 25
  6. Scott Peak Loop 30
  7. North Tahoe City Loop 33
  8. Antone Meadows Loop 37
  9. North Lake Tahoe Regional Park 40
10. Brockway Summit to Tahoe City Point-to-Point 42
11. Brockway Summit to Mount Baldy Out-and-Back 47
12. Tyrolean Point-to-Point 51
13. Tahoe Meadows to Marlette Lake to Flume Trail Point-to-Point 54
14. Flume Trail Loop 60
15. Spooner Summit to South Camp Peak Out-and-Back 64
16. Kingsbury Grade to South Camp Peak Out-and-Back 67
17. Kingsbury Grade to Big Meadow Point-to-Point 71
18. Power Line Loop 74
19. Cold Creek Loop 79
20. Corral Trail Loop 82
21. Armstrong Pass to Saxon Creek Loop 85
22. Big Meadow to Pacific Crest Trail Out-and-Back 88
23. Burnside Lake Out-and-Back 91
24. Hawley Grade Point-to-Point 93
25. Washoe Meadows Out-and-Back 96

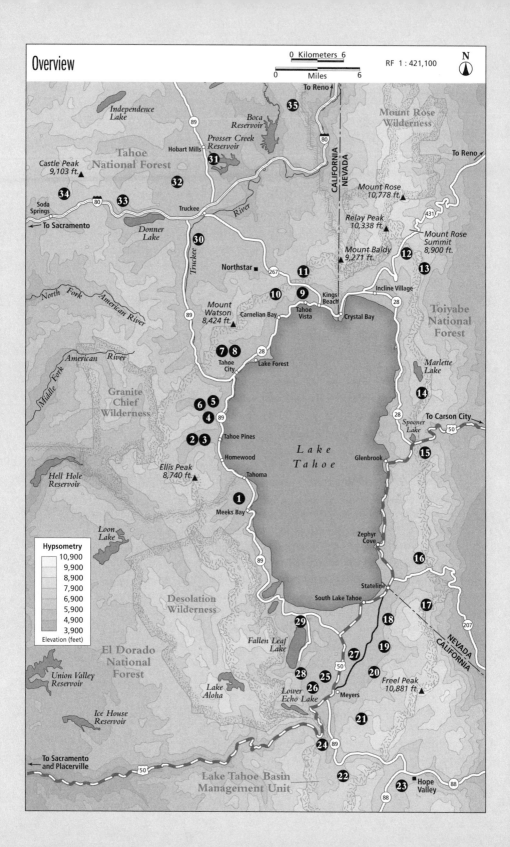

26. Gun Mount Loop 100
27. Upper Truckee River Out-and-Back 104
28. Angora Lakes Out-and-Back 107
29. Fallen Leaf Lake Loop 109

Truckee 113

30. Sawtooth Ridge Trail Loop 114
31. Emigrant Trail to Stampede Reservoir Out-and-Back 118
32. Emigrant Trail to Alder Creek Out-and-Back 122
33. Donner Lake Rim Trail Out-and-Back 125
34. Hole-in-the-Ground Loop 129
35. Verdi Peak Out-and-Back 133

Appendix A: Resources 137
Appendix B: Mountain Bike Parks 138
Appendix C: Paved Bike Paths 139
Appendix D: Campgrounds 141
Appendix E: Lodges 144
Index 145
About the Author 147

Acknowledgments

Appreciation begins with my riding buddies, Jill Nickels, Alan Urena, Deb and Dave Hannaford, Danny Foyer (thanks for the quotes), Rob Nowlain, and Joe Ibis. Thanks for sharing the journey. To Donna Spinnelli and Marylyn Bondlow, your moral and training support was every bit as valuable.

The local bike shops were indispensable in their advice and offerings of favorite routes. Particularly helpful were the directions from The Back Country, Tahoe Sports ltd., CyclePaths, Olympic Bike Shop, and the Village Ski Loft. Additional trail advice was offered by Daryl Alessi, Cory Hannaford, Jay Adams, Michael Moore, and Celia Graterol. Huge thanks to you all!

Special kudos go to the collective of folks that got me to the trailhead and back home safely: To my shuttle drivers, Tamara Williams, Dan Voth, Alex Russell, Fred Jackson, and the Peninsula guys in the white pickup. To the flat tire angels, Mario Gallardo and Mike Joyce, for the trailside assist. To Tyler Sargeant for talking me down the mountain from a series of epic wrong turns and a great adventure. And to Josh and the rest of the crew at Mike's Bikes of San Rafael for averting the dreaded mechanicals.

We all share indebtedness to the land managers and trail builders who keep these trails open for mountain biking. Let's repay them with our stewardship. I appreciate the input and review of Susan Sheffield (Donner Lake Rim Trail Association), Brian Barton (California State Parks), Jim Backus (Tahoe Rim Trail Association), Garrett Villanueva (Lake Tahoe Basin Management Unit), Dean Lutz (Tahoe National Forest), Bill Champion (Lake Tahoe–Nevada State Park) and Kathy Long (North Lake Tahoe Regional Park).

I offer sincere gratitude to Scott Adams for sending me to the top of the mountain and Stephen Stringall for helping me track each course. Credit goes to everyone else at The Globe Pequot Press who had a hand in moving this guidebook through the pipeline, particularly Julie Marsh and Paulette Baker.

Mom and Dad, I couldn't have done this without you. Thanks for instilling a love of nature. As always, my deepest thanks and love to Aaron, Alex, and Jeffrey for being my riding companions, driving the distance every weekend, and living this book with me.

Get Ready to Crank!

Welcome to Lake Tahoe

Get ready to put the mountain into your off-road biking. Lake Tahoe is the land of granite peaks, alpine lakes, crystal clear air (albeit thin), pedal-crunching rocks, and real backcountry. Miles of singletrack will take you through fields of wildflowers, up killer climbs, and on gonzo downhill runs. If you don't carry your bike once in a while, then you aren't mountain biking.

Lake Tahoe is a bike-friendly area. There are plenty of bike shops, bike lanes, and bike paths that make it easy to get around. Two sweet trail systems have been a boon to mountain bikers and a testament to our ability to share the trail. The Tahoe Rim Trail and the emerging Donner Lake Rim Trail offer some of the best singletrack around. Winter sports have also added to the network of trails. Cross-country ski tracks convert nicely to multiuse trails in summer, and Northstar at Tahoe is the largest mountain bike park in northern California.

Many of the trails up here are works in progress, and it's an exciting evolution. As more singletrack becomes accessible to bikers, we can leave some of the dirt roads to the logging trucks, off-highway vehicles, and four-wheel enthusiasts. Only two rides in this book are exclusively dirt roads. It is a challenge to describe routes through the maze of trails crisscrossing the forest. Some are authorized trails; some are not. Many are completely unmarked. Portions of routes will change. It is anticipated that the trails presented here will be around for a while, although some may be rerouted for improvements. Nonetheless, when you start on a ride, bring a good sense of direction—and adventure.

You will encounter a variety of trail surfaces: smooth, hard-packed, soft beds of pine needles, meadow mush, fine powder, and lots of decomposed granite (that's sand to us lay folks). And that's just what's under the rocks . . . all sizes of rocks. It has been said that Tahoe has more rocks than the Rocky Mountains. Full-suspension bikes are the steed of choice, outfitted with wide, grippy tires.

Yes, great trails, challenging climbs, and technical treats make Tahoe a cycling paradise. To top it off is the inspiring landscape. Panoramic views reward every climb. How many ways are there to say "gorgeous view"? Let's start with thirty-five: This guide takes you on thirty-five of the best rides around Lake Tahoe and Truckee. Still, there are more trails out there that don't fit in a pocket guide. Some trails can't handle the traffic, and some have access issues. Some homeowner associations are guarding their turf, and, well, some trails are better left to the locals. Look around and you will find them. Talk to the folks at the local bicycle shops and cycling clubs. They know the remaining gems.

Now for a quick bit of business about bike odometers: Whether you like them or not, they have a place in guidebooks. Some riders may find that these published distances don't agree precisely with their readings. Sorry, but the book is correct—and that's that. Do not get hung up about small differences. Readings will vary depending on the calibration of your odometer, the line you ride, whether you backtrack, or if you take any side trips. Use these mileage cues as guides. Armed with the maps, directions, and descriptions, you should stay on track.

Weather

The best months for mountain biking Lake Tahoe are June through October. With annual snowfall ranging from 18 to 50 feet, the biking season depends on when the snow falls and melts. In some years you may be able to start riding the lower elevations in May or ride through November. You will have to wait until July for a number of rides—when the snow has disappeared from the peaks, the creeks have subsided, and meadow trails have dried out. The general rule is snow clears earlier on the peaks east of the lake than those on the west side.

Not to worry, you can still pack a year's worth of riding in five or six months. Some of the most pleasant riding is after Labor Day, when the traffic has thinned out, the days are still warm and clear, and the nights are crisp.

On average, the sun shines 274 days a year up here—nice. Average summer temperatures at South Lake Tahoe range from 38 to 79 degrees, with less than 2 inches of rain. May and October bring cooler temperatures of 32 to 59 degrees and more precipitation. Be warned; it can snow in any month. The key to comfortable riding is to dress in layers. Even on a sunny day, it can be cold and windy on the mountaintops.

Thunderstorms can pop up in the afternoons during summer, so be prepared with a light rain jacket. If caught in a thunderstorm, get off the ridges, and don't think of hiding under a lone tree. If you are caught in the open, ditch the bike for the duration.

Altitude

You will be riding at elevations between 5,500 and 9,500 feet. If you are not use to the elevation, don't beat yourself up as you gasp for air. Take these special moments to enjoy the scenery. Being in shape doesn't help you acclimate; it can take several days to adjust. If you are coming from sea level, it helps to spend the night at elevation before setting out on the trail. Drink plenty of water, starting before the ride. On the trail, bring a full camelback *and* a water bottle. Symptoms of altitude sickness are similar to the flu—headache, nausea, unusual fatigue, vomiting, and trouble sleeping. Alcohol, sleeping pills, and narcotics can make things worse. If symptoms are severe or persist, particularly after three days, call the doctor.

Remember that you are closer to the sun. It can be piercing on the mountain, so don't spare the sunscreen.

Flora and Fauna

These rides will take you through forests of pine, fir, and cedar mixed with stands of alder and aspen along the creeks. Twisted junipers appear at the higher elevations. An array of wildflowers will infuse their brilliant colors along the way.

These forests have been logged extensively, particularly the Jeffrey and sugar pines, leading to unnaturally dense forests of firs. The less drought- and disease-resistant firs have left thick forests vulnerable to major fires. Aggressive salvage logging is under way and will be seen in the form of large piles of cut debris along some trails.

Tahoe is rich in wildlife, although you may have to be still to notice. This is home to bears, deer, marmots, coyotes, squirrels, bald eagles, hawks, and owls, among many others. Mountain lions are a growing concern for wilderness cyclists, but they are seen only occasionally up here. Their sightings are more likely in the Truckee area or mountains east of Lake Tahoe. I am more concerned about the following hazards:

Black bears are common. Even the brown and blond ones are black bears. In general they are docile and agreeable to sharing their habitat, typically taking any opportunity to avoid conflict with people. If you come upon a bear, don't run or ride. Let it know you are there. Make eye contact, but don't stare. Appreciate the experience, and then move on with respect and self-confidence. If you don't look or smell like garbage, they probably won't be interested.

Mosquitoes: Be prepared for lots of big ones. These hungry buggers thrive in the meadows and along the creeks. Use sunscreen laced with insect repellent, even "where the sun don't shine." Mosquitoes have evolved a proboscis that penetrates Lycra.

Hunters: The sound of gunshots can be a little unnerving for urban folks, particularly when they are in close range. Depending on where you are and who you ask, you may get mixed messages on whether hunting is allowed. In most places, it is not. But in fall, you may hear shots nearby. Wear bright colors, make noise, and ride swiftly.

Wilderness Restrictions and Regulations

Eighty percent of the Lake Tahoe Basin is under public ownership. Most of that is national forestland. The federal land in the Lake Tahoe watershed is managed by the Lake Tahoe Basin Management Unit. Outside the basin, federal land is managed by the Tahoe National Forest and Humboldt-Toiyabe National Forest. California State Parks manages several parks—Sugar Pine Point, Ward Creek, and Burton Creek. Lake Tahoe–Nevada State Park manages the area surrounding the Flume Trail.

There are four specific areas closed to all mountain biking: Desolation Wilderness, Granite Chief Wilderness, Mount Rose Wilderness, and the entire Pacific Crest Trail. These are not negotiable. Mountain bikers are a closely watched group. Be mindful and consider every person you meet on the trail as a potential lobbyist for or against mountain biking. Make sure your encounter will convince them we belong on these trails.

IMBA Rules of the Trail

Thousands of miles of dirt trails have been closed to mountain bicyclists. The irresponsible riding habits of a few riders have been a factor. Do your part to maintain trail access by observing the following rules of the trail, formulated by the International Mountain Bicycling Association (IMBA). IMBA's mission is to promote environmentally sound and socially responsible mountain biking.

1. **Ride on open trails only.** Respect trail and road closures (ask if not sure), avoid possible trespass on private land, obtain permits and authorization as may be required. Federal and state wilderness areas are closed to cycling. The way you ride will influence trail management decisions and policies.

2. **Zero impact.** Be sensitive to the dirt beneath you. Even on open (legal) trails, you should not ride under conditions where you will leave evidence of your passing, such as on certain soils after a rain. Recognize different types of soil and trail construction; practice low-impact cycling. This also means staying on existing trails and not creating any new ones. Be sure to pack out at least as much as you pack in.

3. **Control your bicycle!** Inattention for even a second can cause problems. Obey all bicycle speed regulations and recommendations.

4. **Always yield the trail.** Make known your approach well in advance. A friendly greeting (or bell) is considerate and works well; don't startle others. Show your respect when passing by, slowing to a walking pace or stopping. Anticipate other trail users at corners and blind spots.

5. **Never spook animals.** All animals are startled by an unannounced approach, a sudden movement, or a loud noise. This can be dangerous for you, others, and the animals. Give animals extra room and time to adjust to you. When passing horses, use special care and follow directions from the horseback riders (dismount and ask if uncertain). Running cattle and disturbing wildlife is a serious offense. Leave gates as you found them, or as marked.

6. **Plan ahead.** Know your equipment, your ability, and the area in which you are riding—and prepare accordingly. Be self-sufficient at all times, keep your equipment in good repair, and carry necessary supplies for changes in weather or other conditions. A well-executed trip is a satisfaction to you and not a burden or offense to others. Always wear a helmet.

Keep trails open by setting a good example of environmentally sound and socially responsible off-road cycling. Perhaps you can take it a step further and volunteer for a trail maintenance crew.

Don't let all of these precautions dampen your enthusiasm. Biking this region is great! Just pay attention to yourself, those around you, and the environment.

How to Use This Book

Each region begins with a **Section Intro,** where you're given a sweeping look at the lay of the land. After this general overview, chapters are presented that feature specific rides within that region.

To aid in quick decision-making, each ride chapter begins with a **ride summary.** These short summaries give you a taste of the mountain bike adventure to follow. You'll learn about the trail terrain and what surprises the route has to offer. Next, you'll find the quick, nitty-gritty details of the ride: where the trailhead is located, the length and type of route, estimated riding time, difficulty rating, type of trail terrain, best riding season, what other trail users you may encounter, the land status, the nearest town, trail contacts (for updates on trail conditions), and trail schedules and usage fees.

The **Finding the trailhead** section gives you dependable directions from a nearby city or town right down to where you'll want to park your car. In **Miles and Directions,** we provide mileage cues to identify all turns and trail name changes, as well as points of interest. While it's impossible to cover everything, you can rest assured that we won't miss what's important.

How to Use the Maps

This book uses **Elevation Profiles** to provide an idea of the elevation changes you will encounter along each ride. This, in turn, will help you understand the difficulty of the ride. In the profiles, the vertical axes of the graphs show the total distance climbed in feet. In contrast, the horizontal axes show the distance traveled in miles. It is important to understand that the vertical (feet) and horizontal (miles) scales can differ between rides. Read each profile carefully, making sure you read both the height and distance shown. This will help you interpret what you see in each profile. Some elevation profiles may show gradual ascents and descents to be steep and steep ones to be gradual. Elevation profiles are not provided for rides with little or no elevation gain.

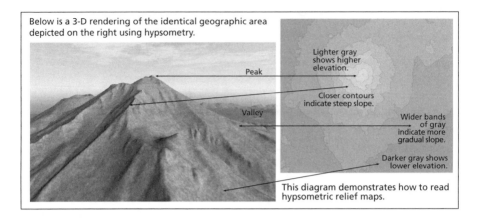

Below is a 3-D rendering of the identical geographic area depicted on the right using hypsometry.

Lighter gray shows higher elevation.

Peak

Closer contours indicate steep slope.

Valley

Wider bands of gray indicate more gradual slope.

Darker gray shows lower elevation.

This diagram demonstrates how to read hypsometric relief maps.

The maps in this book that depict a detailed close-up of an area use elevation tints, called hypsometry, to portray relief. Each gray tone represents a range of equal elevation, as shown in the scale key with the map. These maps will give you a good idea of elevation gain and loss. The darker tones are lower elevations and the lighter grays are higher elevations. The lighter the tone, the higher the elevation. Narrow bands of different gray tones spaced closely together indicate steep terrain, whereas wider bands indicate areas of more gradual slope.

Go Forth

The forty-niners were right; there are treasures in these mountains that will make you rich forever. Just spend some time here and you will find them. Now go out and ride.

Map Legend

Boundaries

National forest boundary

Management unit boundary

Wilderness area boundary

State park boundary

State boundary

Transportation

Interstate

U.S. highway

State highway

Primary road

Paved road

Gravel/dirt road

Unimproved road/ doubletrack

Featured gravel/dirt road

Featured unimproved/ doubletrack

Featured singletrack

Other singletrack

Ski lift

Hydrology

River/creek

Intermittent stream

Lake/river

Marsh/swamp

Physiography

)(Pass

▲ Peak

Symbols

Trailhead

Trail locator

Trail turnaround

Dam

Parking

Airport

Beach

Wildlife area

Snow park

Ski area

Golf course

Cemetery

Mine/gravel pit

Campground

House

School

Picnic area

Town

Viewpoint

Point of Interest

Visitor center

Gate

Bridge

No bikes allowed

Ride Finder

Number	Ride	100% Coveted Singletrack	Not a Bit of Singletrack	Easy Cruise	Moderate Rides	Technical Tests	Real Climbs	Great Downhill	Finest Long Rides
1	General Creek Loop with Out-and-Back to Lost Lake			●			●		
2	Blackwood Canyon to Ellis Lake Out-and-Back						●		
3	Lower Blackwood Canyon Loop			●					
4	Stanford Rock Loop					●	●	●	
5	Page Meadows Double Loop				●				
6	Scott Peak Loop						●	●	
7	North Tahoe City Loop				●			●	
8	Antone Meadows Loop			●					
9	North Lake Tahoe Regional Park	●		●	●				
10	Brockway Summit to Tahoe City Point-to-Point	●				●	●	●	●
11	Brockway Summit to Mount Baldy Out-and-Back	●				●	●	●	
12	Tyrolean Point-to-Point	●						●	
13	Tahoe Meadows to Marlette Lake to Flume Trail Point-to-Point					●	●	●	●
14	Flume Trail Loop				●		●		●
15	Spooner Summit to South Camp Peak Out-and-Back	●					●	●	
16	Kingsbury Grade to South Camp Peak Out-and-Back	●				●			
17	Kingsbury Grade to Big Meadow Point-to-Point	●				●	●		●
18	Power Line Loop				●				
19	Cold Creek Loop				●				

Number	Ride	100% Coveted Singletrack	Not a Bit of Singletrack	Easy Cruise	Moderate Rides	Technical Tests	Real Climbs	Great Downhill	Finest Long Rides
20	Corral Trail Loop				•				
21	Armstrong Pass to Saxon Creek Loop					•	•	•	
22	Big Meadow to Pacific Crest Trail Out-and-Back	•			•				
23	Burnside Lake Out-and-Back		•		•				
24	Hawley Grade Point-to-Point	•				•		•	
25	Washoe Meadows Out-and-Back			•					
26	Gun Mount Loop				•				
27	Upper Truckee River Out-and-Back			•					
28	Angora Lakes Out-and-Back				•				
29	Fallen Leaf Lake Loop			•					
30	Sawtooth Ridge Trail Loop	•			•				
31	Emigrant Trail to Stampede Reservoir Out-and-Back	•		•					
32	Emigrant Trail to Alder Creek Out-and-Back	•		•					
33	Donner Lake Rim Trail Out-and-Back						•	•	
34	Hole-in-the-Ground Loop					•		•	
35	Verde Peak Out-and-Back		•				•		

Lake Tahoe

California and Nevada share Lake Tahoe, the crown jewel of the Sierra Nevada range. Its stats are impressive: 22 miles long, 12 miles wide, and 72 miles of shoreline. The lake's surface sits at 6,225 feet, from which all rides rise above. The crystal blue lake attracts a growing number of visitors and residents each year. During summer, the beaches and casinos at the south end of the lake draw the most traffic. Never mind the congestion; you can quickly escape the masses on your mountain bike.

The Tahoe Rim Trail frames the riding and features some of the best singletrack and dramatic views around. This spectacular 164-mile trail encircles the entire Lake Tahoe Basin; about 60 percent of the trail is sweet singletrack that is accessible to cyclists. This hasn't always been the case, so please do your part to keep it that way. The climbing and technical challenges make riding the rim a rewardingly moderate to difficult journey.

Tahoe is not all epic rides; it offers something for everyone. Between the lake and the rising mountains, there are plenty of easy and moderate rides close to town. Some of these can be reached directly from local bike paths.

Folks generally refer to Lake Tahoe in three sectors: (1) North Shore—Tahoe City, Kings Beach, and Incline Village; (2) South Shore and the developed towns of South Lake Tahoe and Stateline; and (3) West Shore—the collection of small towns running from Tahoe City to Emerald Bay. Since trails aren't neatly confined to each sector, the trails in this guide have been listed clockwise around the lake.

1 General Creek Loop with Out-and-Back to Lost Lake

The General Creek area offers something for all abilities; you can simply turn around at any point. Begin at Sugar Pine Point State Park Campground and cruise up the canyon on a well-graded dirt road. At 2.0 miles, where the road crosses General Creek for the return of the short loop option, a gorgeous singletrack heads into the woods. What begins as a well-packed trail becomes progressively steep, technical, and secluded as it follows General Creek up the lush canyon. In places, the alders are in your face. Nearly 5 miles into the ride the trail crosses the creek, where there are some nice upstream pools. From there, a quarter-mile of steep hike-a-bike takes you up to the rutted and overgrown Forest Service road leading to Lost Lake. Along the way, the views of Lake Tahoe are striking. Since bikes are not allowed in designated wilderness areas, this is as close to the Desolation Wilderness as you can get. While this is a great spot to camp, a trailer would not make it up the hike-a-bike.

Start: From the entrance to Sugar Pine Point State Park Campground
Distance: General Creek Loop, 5.0 miles; full out-and-back to Lost Lake, 14.5 miles
Approximate riding time: General Creek Loop, 30 minutes; Lost Lake, 2½ hours
Difficulty rating: Easy nontechical loop; moderate to difficult, strenuous and technical out-and-back that includes rugged hike-a-bike
Trail surface: Dirt road, singletrack, and paved bike path and campground road
Seasons: June through October
Other trail users: Hikers; no dogs allowed
Land status: Sugar Pine Point State Park;

Lake Tahoe Basin Management Unit
Nearest town: Tahoma, California
Fees and permits: $6.00 parking fee
Schedule: Daylight hours only
Maps: Maptech CD: California, High Sierra/Tahoe; USGS maps: Meeks Bay, CA; Homewood, CA
Trail contacts: Sugar Pine Point State Park, California Highway 89, Tahoma, CA 96142; (530) 525-7232; www.parks.ca.gov. Lake Tahoe Basin Management Unit, USDA Forest Service, 35 College Drive, South Lake Tahoe, CA 96150; (530) 543-2600; www.fs.fed.us/r5/ltbmu.

Finding the trailhead: From Tahoe City, take CA 89 south for just over 9 miles. Turn right into the entrance to Sugar Pine Point State Park Campground. There is a fee parking lot just left of the ranger's kiosk. Pick up a campground map to help find the trailhead. There are restrooms and water at the campground.

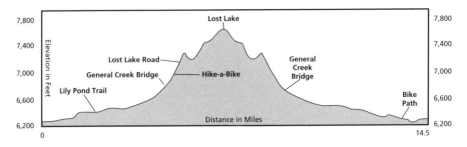

General Creek Loop with Out-and-Back to Lost Lake

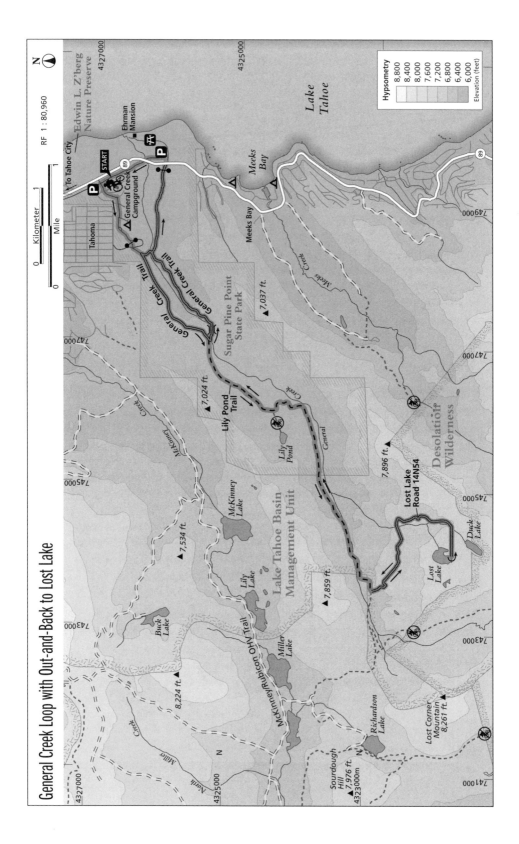

From South Lake Tahoe, take CA 89 north 17.5 miles to the campground entrance on the west side of the highway. **Trailhead GPS:** N 39 03.47, W 120 07.36

Miles and Directions

0.0 **START** at the entrance kiosk to Sugar Pine Point State Park Campground. Ride west on the paved road through the campground to Campsites 149 and 150.

0.8 At the gate between Campsites 149 and 159, start on the unsigned General Creek Trail—a wide dirt road.

1.1 Continue straight where the road forks, following the signs to Lily Pond and Lost Lake. (**Option:** For a shorter loop, turn left and cross the bridge over General Creek.)

1.4 Continue straight, ignoring the road on the right.

2.1 Turn right onto the singletrack where the sign notes the end of the park's Red Trail. This begins the out-and-back to Lost Lake. Stay on the main trail, ignoring any side trails. Bikes are not allowed up to Lily Pond. (**General Creek Loop Option:** Turn left on the dirt road and pick up directions at Mile 11.7 below.)

4.2 The trail becomes steeper and rockier. Veer right up the hill where vague trails wander over to the creek. Most of the trail is rideable, although you may need to walk some spots.

4.8 Arrive at a battered wooden post and a fork in the trail. Turn left and cautiously cross General Creek. Beware of mammoth mosquitoes. Once across the creek, veer right up a narrow trail through thick brush. You are climbing up a rocky gorge, wondering why you brought your bike. Your mileage may be a little vague through here, since you are ferrying your bike.

5.0 Once off the rocks, turn left onto the dirt road to Lost Lake. (**Option:** Turn right and head for the McKinney/Rubicon Trail, with a series of lakes along the way. This boulder-strewn road is a premier off-road vehicle route and will eventually take you to CA 89. From there, turn right onto the bike path back to the campground.)

6.6 Pass Duck Lake on the left.

6.9 Arrive at Lost Lake. Kick back and enjoy the high country. When you are ready, turn around and retrace your tracks.

8.7 Turn right for the steep decent over the granite slabs. (**Option:** Continue straight for a second chance to check out the rugged McKinney/Rubicon Trail.)

9.0 Cross the creek and turn right.

11.7 Arrive back at the dirt road. Turn right and cross over the bridge.

12.7 Continue straight at the fork. (**Shortcut:** Turn left, cross General Creek on the bridge, and return to the campground.)

13.7 Pass the gate, cross CA 89, and head for the entrance to Sugar Pine Point Picnic Area. Immediately turn left onto the paved bike route. (**Option:** Cruise into the picnic area and check out the historic Ehrman Mansion.)

13.9 Follow the bike route across CA 89 and back to the campground entrance. You will cross another access trail to the mansion and beach along the way; just continue north.

14.4 Turn left into the campground.

14.5 Arrive at the entrance station where you began.

2 Blackwood Canyon to Ellis Lake Out-and-Back

This ride follows the paved Blackwood Canyon Road up to Barker Pass before tackling a steep singletrack climb to Ellis Lake. There are plenty of options for exploring the dirt roads throughout Blackwood Canyon and the adjoining McKinney/Rubicon Canyon to the south, but most of them are best left to off-highway vehicles. With the increasing miles of singletrack in Tahoe, why eat someone else's dust? Avoiding that, this beautiful ride takes you to up to stellar views of the Desolation Wilderness and the El Dorado National Forest.

The initial 7.0 miles of paved road is nontechnical, but a steady gain of 1,500 feet. You can skip the road ride and start at the trailhead to Ellis Lake. The first mile of singletrack is insanely steep. While this section is best for hiking, it's also for people who don't attempt a summit without their bike. Be prepared to push your bike, knowing it would be easier without the extra baggage. Once on the ridge, you will pass through a garden of wildflowers with sweeping views in all directions.

Start: From the gated entrance to Blackwood Canyon
Distance: 19.4-mile out-and-back
Approximate riding time: 3 to 4 hours
Difficulty rating: Difficult—long and steep climb with rough sections of rock, some unrideable
Trail surface: 70 percent paved road, 26 percent singletrack, and 4 percent dirt road
Seasons: Late June through October; much earlier on Blackwood Canyon Road
Other trail users: Vehicles and hikers

Land status: Lake Tahoe Basin Management Unit
Nearest town: Tahoe City, California
Fees and permits: No fees or permits required
Schedule: 24 hours a day
Maps: Maptech CD: California, High Sierra/Tahoe; USGS map: Homewood, CA
Trail contacts: Lake Tahoe Basin Management Unit, USDA Forest Service, 35 College Drive, South Lake Tahoe, CA 96150; (530) 543-2600; www.fs.fed.us/r5/ltbmu

Finding the trailhead: From Tahoe City, drive 4 miles south on California Highway 89 to Blackwood Canyon Road, where you turn right (west). The mileage for this ride begins at the gate near the signs for the Blackwood Canyon Sno-Park. The entrance to Kaspian Bicycle Campground is on the right just before the gate. There is parking and an outhouse at the campground. **Trailhead GPS:** N 39 06.80, W 120 09.55

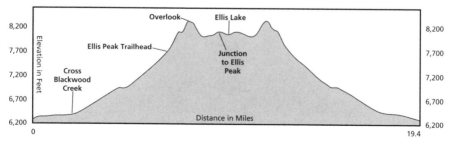

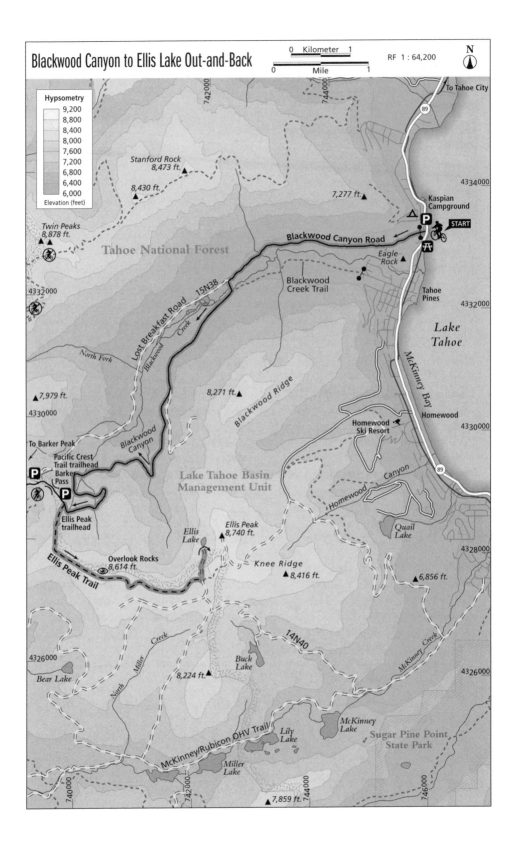

Blackwood Canyon to Ellis Lake Out-and-Back

0 Kilometer 1

0 Mile 1

RF 1 : 64,200

N

Hypsometry

	9,200
	8,800
	8,400
	8,000
	7,600
	7,200
	6,800
	6,400
	6,000

Elevation (feet)

742000

744000

To Tahoe City

89

Stanford Rock
8,473 ft. ▲

4334000

8,430 ft. ▲

7,277 ft. ▲

Kaspian
Campground

Twin Peaks
8,878 ft.

Tahoe National Forest

START

P

Blackwood Canyon Road

Eagle
Rock

4332000

Lost Breakfast Road 15N38

Blackwood
Creek Trail

Tahoe
Pines

4332000

North Fork

Blackwood Creek

Lake
Tahoe

McKinney Bay

7,979 ft. ▲

8,271 ft. ▲

Blackwood Ridge

4330000

To Barker Peak

Blackwood Canyon

Homewood

Homewood
Ski Resort

Homewood

4330000

Pacific Crest
Trail trailhead
Barker
Pass

P

89

P

Lake Tahoe Basin
Management Unit

Homewood Canyon

Quail
Lake

Ellis Peak
trailhead

Ellis
Lake

Ellis Peak
8,740 ft. ▲

4328000

Ellis Peak Trail

Overlook Rocks
8,614 ft.

Knee Ridge

8,416 ft. ▲

6,856 ft. ▲

North Miller Creek

14N40

McKinney Creek

4326000

Bear Lake

8,224 ft. ▲

Buck
Lake

4326000

McKinney
Lake

McKinney/Rubicon OHV Trail

Lily
Lake

Sugar Pine Point
State Park

Miller
Lake

740000

742000

744000

746000

7,859 ft. ▲

Riding on the edge

Option: There are several places to begin along Blackwood Canyon Road. The trailhead to Ellis Peak and Ellis Lake is at the end of the pavement near Barker Pass. **Trailhead GPS:** N 39 04.31, W 120 12.87

Miles and Directions

0.0   **START** from the gate on Blackwood Canyon Road and follow the pavement all the way to the summit of Barker Pass.

2.2   Veer left to stay on the paved road at a fork with the off-road vehicle route. The road soon crosses Blackwood Creek.

2.4   Just past the river, the climb begins.

6.8   Reach the end of the pavement. For most, this is a good spot to turn around. For the undeterred, turn left and head up the singletrack to Ellis Lake. (**Option:** Continue straight for 0.5 mile to the parking area for the Pacific Crest Trail. Quash any thoughts of poaching that one. Ride through the parking lot, past the gas tanks on the right, and pick up the single lane Forest Road 15N38 down to Blackwood Canyon Road. In the old Tahoe-Roubaix Course, this was known as Lost Breakfast Road.)

7.4   You are out of the woods and riding the narrow divide that drops sharply to Blackwood Canyon on the left. An expansive view of Desolation Wilderness opens up to the southeast. If you time it right, you will be surrounded by wildflowers.

7.8   Unless you are going the full distance to Ellis Peak, this is the best view—and another sane place to turn around. The trail will start descending up ahead.

9.2 Ignore the spur trail on the left to a small pond.

9.3 Turn left at the intersection to Ellis Lake. (**Option:** Continue straight up the singletrack to Ellis Peak. About half of this is rideable. Consider stashing your bike and hiking to the peak. You will connect with a dirt road near the summit. Keep to the left to reach the end of the road. The last stretch is a steep hike up the rocky peak to an inspiring view.)

9.7 Arrive at the lake and ride to the far end for a view of the valley below. Look up the cliffs towering over the lake and decide if you want to go the distance to Ellis Peak. If you don't, this is the turnaround point. Retrace your tracks home.

12.6 Depending on how much exploring you did around the lake, you will reach the trailhead and the end of the singletrack. Turn right for the descent down Blackwood Canyon Road. Heads up for cars.

17.1 (**Option:** The unsigned Blackwood Creek Trail is at the bottom of the downhill before the road crosses Blackwood Creek. Turn right and follow the singletrack through the woods. This will drop you onto Grand Avenue and eventually to the West Lake Bike Path. Turn left and head back to Blackwood Canyon Road.)

19.4 Arrive back at the start.

3 Lower Blackwood Canyon Loop

Here's an easy, level ride for beginners. Join the skateboarders and in-line skaters for the 2.0-mile ride along the paved and tree-lined Blackwood Canyon Road. Just before the climb to Barker Pass, this loop bails onto a sweet singletrack that runs downstream along the south side of Blackwood Creek. The path starts with some hefty whoop-de-dos to break up the pace. After a smooth meander through the quiet woods, the trail ends in a neighborhood and eventually spills onto the West Lake Bike Path. The return along the lake's edge takes you to a great picnic spot, complete with a table.

Start: From the gated entrance to Blackwood Canyon Road

Distance: 5.1-mile loop

Approximate riding time: 30 to 45 minutes

Difficulty rating: Easy—level and smooth surface

Trail surface: 55 percent paved road, 20 percent singletrack, 13 percent paved bike path, and 12 percent dirt road

Seasons: June through October

Other trail users: Vehicles, hikers, and skaters

Land status: Lake Tahoe Basin Management Unit

Nearest town: Tahoe City, California

Fees and permits: No fees or permits required

Schedule: 24 hours a day

Maps: Maptech CD: California, High Sierra/Tahoe; USGS map: Homewood, CA

Trail contacts: Lake Tahoe Basin Management Unit, USDA Forest Service, 35 College Drive, South Lake Tahoe, CA 96150; (530) 543-2600; www.fs.fed.us/r5/ltbmu

◀ *Destination—Ellis Lake*

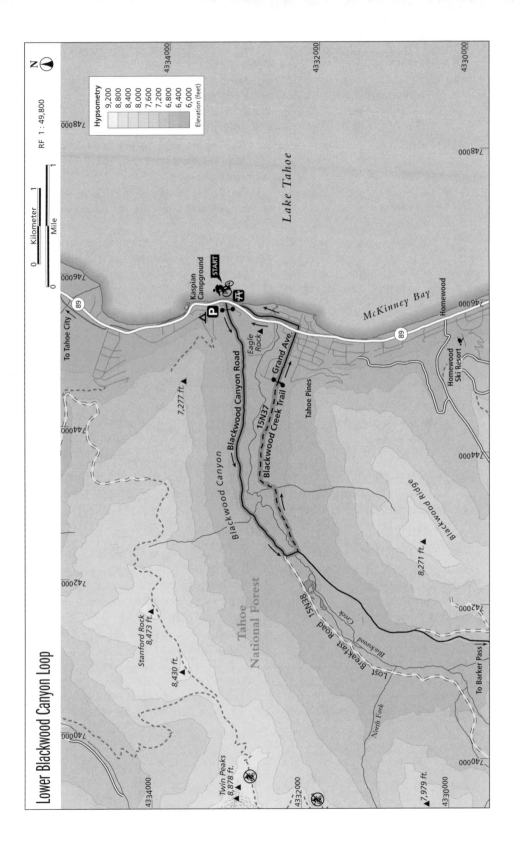

Wrapping up along the West Lake Bike Path

Finding the trailhead: From Tahoe City, drive 4.0 miles south on California Highway 89 to Blackwood Canyon Road. Turn right; the mileage for this ride begins at the gate near the signs for the Blackwood Canyon Sno-Park. The entrance to Kaspian Bicycle Campground is on the right just before the gate. There is parking and an outhouse at the campground. **Trailhead GPS:** N 39 06.80, W 120 09.55

Miles and Directions

0.0 **START** from the gate on Blackwood Canyon Road and ride the pavement up the canyon.

2.2 Veer left to stay on the paved road at the junction with the off-road vehicle route. The road soon crosses Blackwood Creek.

2.3 Turn left on the unsigned Blackwood Canyon Trail. This narrow trail is just before the road bends right for the climb to Barker Pass.

2.7 Veer right at the fork. The spur trail on the left heads to the creek.

2.8 Veer left at the fork.

3.3 Cross the stream and ride between the posts onto Forest Road 15N37.

3.8 Pass the gate and continue straight on Grand Avenue.

4.3 Carefully cross CA 89, turn left onto the West Lake Bike Path, and ride back along the edge of Lake Tahoe. There is a picnic table up ahead and great places to stop along the shoreline.

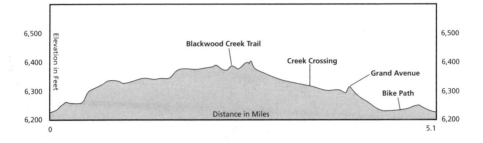

5.0 Cross back over CA 89 and return up Blackwood Canyon.

5.1 Arrive back at the starting gate.

4 Stanford Rock Loop

An easy meander along Ward Creek offers a warm-up before tackling the climb toward Stanford Rock. Catch dramatic views of Blackwood Canyon along the rocky ridge to the summit. The trail skirts the actual peak of Stanford Rock, a mound of rocks not fit for riding. At the crest of the loop, views shift to Twin Peaks, Ward Peak, and the back side of Alpine Meadows Ski Area. The edge of the Granite Chief Wilderness towers overhead as the ride connects with the Tahoe Rim Trail and descends through a steep gorge and meadows of wildflowers. Expect sharp-edged water bars, rocky steps, water crossings, and more rocks on the downhill run. Save this one for late summer and fall when the snow is gone, the creeks subside, and the meadows dry out.

Start: From Ward Creek and California Highway 89

Distance: 13.5-mile loop

Approximate riding time: 2 to 3 hours

Difficulty rating: Difficult—strenuous climb and steep, rocky descent

Trail surface: 82 percent singletrack, 13 percent dirt road, and 5 percent paved road

Seasons: July through October

Other trail users: Hikers and equestrians; no dogs allowed in Ward Creek State Park

Land status: Lake Tahoe Basin Management Unit

Nearest town: Tahoe City, California

Fees and permits: No fees or permits required

Schedule: Daylight hours only in Ward Creek State Park

Maps: Maptech CD: California, High Sierra/Tahoe; USGS maps: Tahoe City, CA; Homewood, CA; Tahoe Rim Trail, Barker Pass to Tahoe City Segment; Lake Tahoe Trail Map, Adventure Maps, Inc., 2005

Trail contacts: Lake Tahoe Basin Management Unit, USDA Forest Service, 35 College Drive, South Lake Tahoe, CA 96150; (530) 543-2600; www.fs.fed.us/r5/ltbmu. California State Parks, P.O. Box 266, Tahoma, CA 96142; (530) 525-7232; www.parks.ca.gov. Tahoe Rim Trail Association, 948 Incline Way, Incline Village, NV 89451; (775) 298-0012; www.tahoerimtrail.org.

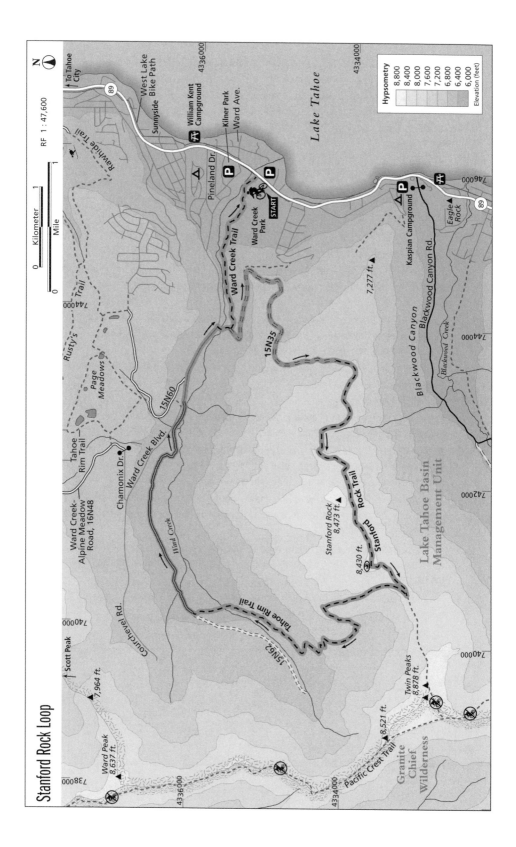

Stanford Rock Loop

RF 1 : 47,600

Hypsometry

8,800
8,400
8,000
7,600
7,200
6,800
6,400
6,000

Elevation (feet)

Lake Tahoe

To Tahoe City

89

West Lake
Sunnyside Bike Path

William Kent Campground

Kilner Park
Ward Ave.

Pineland Dr.

Ward Creek Trail

Ward Creek Park

START

Rawhide Trail

7,277 ft.

15N35

Blackwood Canyon

Blackwood Canyon Rd.

Kaspian Campground

Eagle Rock

Blackwood Creek

Lake Tahoe Basin
Management Unit

15N60

Page Meadows

Rusty's Trail

Tahoe Rim Trail

Chamonix Dr.

Ward Creek-
Alpine Meadow
Road, 16N48

Ward Creek Blvd.

Ward Creek

Stanford Rock
8,473 ft.

8,430 ft.

Stanford Rock Trail

Tahoe Rim Trail

15N62

Courchevel Rd.

Scott Peak
7,964 ft.

Ward Peak
8,637 ft.

Twin Peaks
8,878 ft.

8,521 ft.

Granite Chief
Wilderness

Pacific Crest Trail

N

0   1   Kilometer

0   1   Mile

Finding the trailhead: From Tahoe City, drive 5 miles south on CA 89. The ride begins just past Ward Avenue and the Black Bear Tavern. The trailhead is off the West Lake Bike Path just south of the bridge over Ward Creek. There is limited parking on the east side of the road. There is more parking, water, and restrooms at Kilner Park on the corner of Ward Avenue and CA 89. **Trailhead GPS:** N 39 07.94, W 120 09.49

Miles and Directions

0.0 **START** on the trail that is simply signed STATE PARK PROPERTY. You are heading into Ward Creek State Park. The well-traveled trail follows the creek for over a mile; ignore the side trails on the right to the creek.

0.2 Veer left at the fork, then make a sharp right in 150 yards at a vague T intersection.

0.5 Continue straight at the trail crossing.

1.3 Veer left as the trail splits, and immediately veer left again onto another unsigned single-track. At the end of the ride, you will complete the loop from the right after crossing Ward Creek.

1.4 Turn left up the unsigned Stanford Rock Trail. The climb is steady for the next 4.0 miles through forest and occasional meadows. The trail starts out as a singletrack path worn through an overgrown jeep road, Forest Road 15N35.

3.8 A view of Lake Tahoe and McKinney Bay appears through the trees on the left as the trail levels off for a brief respite.

4.3 At a small clearing, ride to the overlook of Blackwood Canyon, Ellis Peak, and Barker Pass before veering right to continue the climb. There are more panoramic views up ahead as the trail gets rockier and steeper.

5.3 As the trail levels off, look up to the right through the trees for a pile of rocks; this is Stanford Rock. (**Side trip:** Hide the bike and hike to the peak; it's a rough scramble with bike cleats and other great views are up ahead.)

5.9 Arrive at the overlook for a view of Twin Peaks and the ridge of the Granite Chief Wilderness. Lower your seat now; the ride home is all downhill. Brace for loose and rocky sections.

6.4 Turn right onto the Tahoe Rim Trail to Ward Canyon. Get ready for the countless rock water bars and steps. Great effort has been made to channel the water draining down the hillside.

8.1 Stop for a good look at the waterfall; you can't look and hope to make this turn.

9.1 Cross the stream, and veer left at the top of the bank.

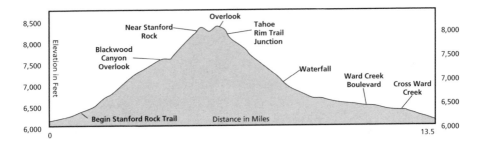

9.6 After crossing another creekbed, the trail widens into a rocky dirt road.

11.3 Turn right onto Ward Creek Boulevard.

12.0 Turn right onto the gravel at the split-rail fence, go around the gate, and pick your way across Ward Creek. On the other side, find the narrow singletrack up the steep bank and through a tunnel of brush. (**Option:** If you don't want to ford Ward Creek, particularly when the water is high and cold, continue down the paved road. Follow the yellow stripe to CA 89, where you turn right on the paved bike path back to the start.)

12.2 Turn left to complete the loop section of the ride, and retrace your tracks to the trailhead.

13.1 Remember to veer left sharply and then right to follow the main trail.

13.5 Arrive back at the starting point.

5 Page Meadows Double Loop

There are several ways to reach the popular Page Meadows—a series of interconnecting meadows with views of the lofty peaks along the eastern edge of the Granite Chief Wilderness. This route up Ward Canyon has the smoothest climb and best singletrack. For some, these advantages may be offset by the distance on the pavement. Beginners wanting a no-climb route can access the meadows from the Pineland neighborhood. With a maze of trails and no signs, Page Meadows is great for exploring or getting lost, whichever way you view it. The trails are rocky and loose in sections and pass through more forest than meadow. While the trails outside the meadow are rideable early in the season, stay out of the meadows until they have dried out. The meadows are being restored after years of free-riding off-road vehicles. Lather up with sunscreen for the ride up Ward Canyon and bug repellent for the cruise through the meadow.

Start: From the intersection of Pineland Drive and California Highway 89

Distance: 13.1-mile double loop

Approximate riding time: 1½ to 2 hours

Difficulty rating: Moderate—steady climbing and uneven terrain

Trail surface: 42 percent singletrack, 30 percent paved road, 18 percent dirt road, 10 percent paved bike path

Seasons: Perimeter loop, June through October; Page Meadows trails, wait until July. Check at the local bike shops for conditions in the meadow before heading in.

Other trail users: Hikers, equestrians, and vehicles

Land status: Lake Tahoe Basin Management Unit

Nearest town: Tahoe City, California

Fees and permits: No fees or permits required

Schedule: 24 hours a day

Maps: Maptech CD: California, High Sierra/Tahoe; USGS map: Tahoe City, CA; Tahoe Rim Trail, Barker Pass to Tahoe City Segment

Trail contacts: Lake Tahoe Basin Management Unit, USDA Forest Service, 35 College Drive, South Lake Tahoe, CA 96150; (530) 543-2600; www.fs.fed.us/r5/ltbmu. Tahoe Rim Trail Association, 948 Incline Way, Incline Village, NV 89451; (775) 298-0012; www.tahoerimtrail.org.

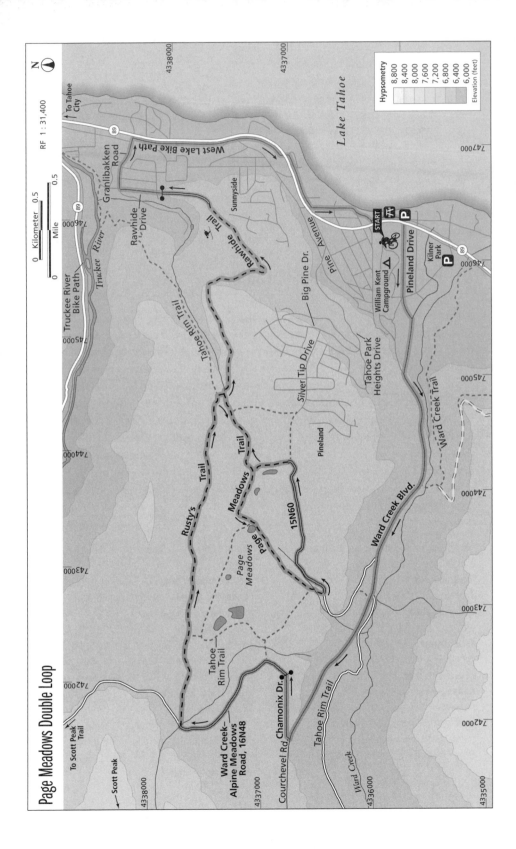

Crossing Page Meadows

Finding the trailhead: From Tahoe City, go south on CA 89 for 2.3 miles. The ride begins at the corner of Pineland Drive, just past William Kent Campground. There is parking along the road and restrooms and water at the campground. **Trailhead GPS:** N 39 08.26, W 120 09.27

Miles and Directions

0.0 **START** from California Highway 89 and ride west up Pineland Drive.

0.4 Veer left at the fork onto Twin Peak Road, following the sign to Ward Valley. This turns into Ward Creek Boulevard.

3.0 Turn right up Chamonix Road.

3.2 At the cul-de-sac, ride around the gate to Forest Road 16N48 and take the singletrack shortcut to the right of the dirt road. In about 125 yards, turn right where the path reconnects with FR 16N48, also called the Ward Creek–Alpine Meadow Road.

4.1 Turn right at the fork on the unsigned Rusty's Trail. Sections of this narrow singletrack are rocky and loose, with body-piercing chamise lining your way.

4.8 Continue straight where the trail becomes part of the Tahoe Rim Trail. (**Option:** A right turn toward Ward Creek will take you toward the upper end of the meadows and one of the last areas to dry out.)

6.1 Turn right toward Page Meadows. After crossing the creek and a brief climb, make a sharp right turn onto the unsigned Page Meadows Trail.

Staying on the trail through fragile Page Meadows

6.2   Continue straight where a singletrack merges from the left.

6.6   Veer left at the fork.

6.7   This is the beginning of the unsigned Page Meadows Loop. Turn right onto the concrete-lattice pathway across the meadow.

6.8   Continue straight where a trail merges from the right.

7.0   Continue straight at the junction. You will soon exit the meadow and weave through the woods to the Tahoe Rim Trail. (**Option:** The trail to the right will take you back toward Rusty's Trail.)

7.5   Turn left briefly onto the Tahoe Rim Trail (TRT). In 50 yards, turn left onto a rocky jeep trail. (**Bailout:** Continue straight on the TRT to Ward Creek Boulevard.)

8.3   Ignore the singletrack on the left that is posted NO MOTORIZED VEHICLES.

8.4   Turn left at the wooden posts and head back toward the meadow.

8.6   This completes the loop of the meadow. Backtrack straight ahead; unless you want to explore, ignore the side trails along the way.

9.1   Continue straight on the unsigned Rawhide Trail at the connector to the TRT. This is an easy junction to miss, and you might blow by it without noticing. Just 100 feet beyond the junction, veer left at the fork. (**Option:** For a technical downhill to Tahoe City, make the sharp left turn at the connector, backtracking to the Tahoe Rim Trail.)

9.3   Veer left as a spur trail heads off on the right to the Pineland neighborhood.

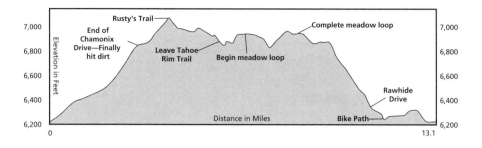

9.7 Continue downhill, ignoring a singletrack heading uphill on the left. There will be many more side trails along the way—ignore them all and stay on the main track.

10.3 Veer right at the fork as the trail widens into an unimproved road.

10.9 Ride past the green gate and continue straight into the neighborhood on Rawhide Drive.

11.1 Turn right onto Granlibakken Road.

11.4 Turn right onto the West Lake Bike Path along CA 89, and follow it back to the start.

12.6 Follow the BIKE ROUTE sign and turn left onto Sequoia Avenue. You will ride down near the lake and past a private beach. The bike path resumes at William Kent Beach.

13.1 Arrive back at the corner of Pineland Drive.

Alternate routes into Page Meadows

Silver Tip Drive: This is the easiest access. Turn west onto Pine Avenue from CA 89. Turn right onto Tahoe Park Heights Drive and then right again at Big Pine Drive. Make a left turn onto Silver Tip Drive. A path leads into the meadow from the end of the road.

Rawhide Drive entrance: Start up the Rawhide Trail at the end of Rawhide Drive. Access is from Granlibakken Road off CA 89.

6 Scott Peak Loop

A trip to Scott Peak makes a challenging extension of a ride to Page Meadows. The Scott Peak Trail is an out-and-back from Forest Road 16N48, the connector between Ward Creek and Alpine Meadows. Once a four-wheel-drive road, the trail is now overgrown and offers a well-graded climb to the top of the Alpine Meadows ski area. The last mile becomes steeper, more technical, and pure singletrack. From the summit you can see the Squaw Valley ski area, Ward Peak, and Twin Peaks. The 8.0-mile descent skirts Page Meadows and tracks the Tahoe Rim Trail down to the Truckee River. The last 1.5 mile of drop is a steep mix of hard-packed trail and loose rocks, with some rock steps along the way. Once in town, it's a smooth ride on the West Lake Bike Path back to the start.

Start: From the intersection of Pineland Drive and California Highway 89
Distance: 17.8-mile loop
Approximate riding time: 2½ hours
Difficulty rating: Difficult—steep and rocky terrain
Trail surface: 50 percent singletrack, 21 percent dirt road, 18 percent paved road, and 11 percent paved bike path
Seasons: Late June through October
Other trail users: Hikers and equestrians
Land status: Lake Tahoe Basin Management Unit

Nearest town: Tahoe City, California
Fees and permits: No fees or permits required
Schedule: 24 hours a day
Maps: Maptech CD: California, High Sierra/Tahoe; USGS map: Tahoe City, CA; Tahoe Rim Trail, Barker Pass to Tahoe City Segment
Trail contacts: Lake Tahoe Basin Management Unit, USDA Forest Service, 35 College Drive, South Lake Tahoe, CA 96150; (530) 543-2600; www.fs.fed.us/r5/ltbmu. Tahoe Rim Trail Association, Incline Village, NV; (775) 298-0012; www.tahoerimtrail.org.

Finding the trailhead: From Tahoe City, go south on CA 89 for 2.3 miles. The ride begins at the corner of Pineland Drive, just past William Kent Campground. There is parking along the road and restrooms and water at the campground. **Trailhead GPS:** N 39 08.26, W 120 09.27

Miles and Directions

0.0 **START** from CA 89 and ride west up Pineland Drive.

0.4 Veer left at the fork on Twin Peak Road, following the sign to Ward Valley. This soon turns into Ward Creek Boulevard.

3.0 Turn right up Chamonix Road.

3.2 At the cul-de-sac, ride around the gate to Forest Road 16N48 and take the singletrack shortcut to the right of the dirt road. In about 125 yards, turn right where the path reconnects with FR 16N48, also called the Ward Creek–Alpine Meadow Road.

4.1 Veer left at the fork and expect a rockier ride. You will complete the out-and-back to Scott Peak here and turn right toward Page Meadows on the way down.

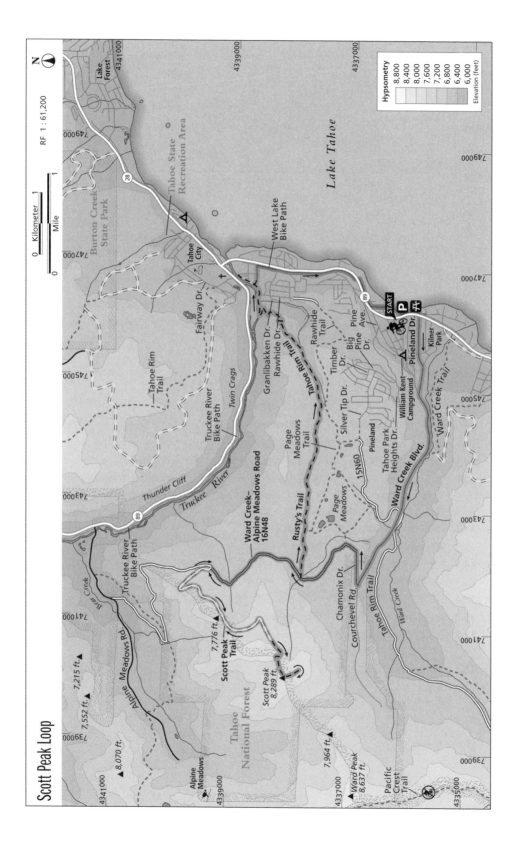

Scott Peak Loop

RF 1 : 61,200

N

0 Kilometer 1
0 Mile 1

Hypsometry

Elevation (feet)
8,800
8,400
8,000
7,600
7,200
6,800
6,400
6,000

Lake Forest

Burton Creek State Park

28

Tahoe State Recreation Area

Tahoe City

Fairway Dr.

Tahoe Rim Trail

Truckee River Bike Path

Twin Crags

West Lake Bike Path

Lake Tahoe

Granlibakken Dr.

Rawhide Dr.

Tahoe Rim Trail

Rawhide Trail

Timber Dr.

Big Pine Dr.

Pine Ave.

START

P

Silver Tip Dr.

Pineland

William Kent Campground

Pineland Dr.

Kilner Park

Page Meadows Trail

Ward Creek Blvd.

Ward Creek Trail

Tahoe Park Heights Dr.

15N60

Page Meadows

Rusty's Trail

Ward Creek-Alpine Meadows Road 16N48

Thunder Cliff

Truckee River

89

Bear Creek

Truckee River Bike Path

Chamonix Dr.

Courchevel Rd.

Ward Creek

Tahoe Rim Trail

7,776 ft.

Scott Peak Trail

Scott Peak 8,289 ft.

Alpine Meadows Rd.

7,215 ft.

7,552 ft.

8,070 ft.

Alpine Meadows

Tahoe National Forest

7,964 ft.

Ward Peak 8,637 ft.

Pacific Crest Trail

4341000

4339000

4337000

4335000

739000

741000

743000

745000

747000

749000

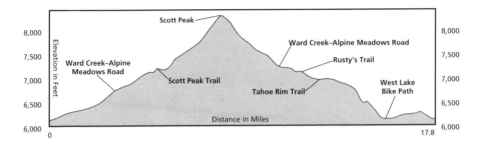

5.4 Turn left at the fork on the unsigned Scott Peak Trail. The road soon becomes overgrown and turns into nice singletrack. (**Option:** Continue straight to Alpine Meadows Road. From there, turn right until you come to the Truckee River Bike Path. Follow the bike path into Tahoe City.)

7.0 Veer right on the main trail; ignore the rogue path on the left.

7.7 Veer left at the fork. (**Quick side trip:** Turn right to check out the view from the ledge.)

7.8 Veer left at the fork, heading toward the ski hut. It may be unlocked, offering a sheltered view of Alpine Meadows and Squaw Valley ski resorts. Continue to the end of the singletrack.

8.0 Lake Tahoe, Twin Peaks (to the south), and Ward Peak (to the west) stand before you. This is the turnaround point.

8.1 Veer right at the fork to retrace your tracks.

10.5 Turn right back onto Ward Creek–Alpine Meadow Road.

11.8 Turn left at the fork onto the unsigned Rusty's Trail.

12.5 Continue straight where the trail becomes part of the Tahoe Rim Trail (TRT).

13.7 Veer left to continue on the TRT to Tahoe City. Set up for loose rocks and rock steps up ahead. (**Option:** Turn right for a cruise through Page Meadows. See Page Meadows Double Loop for more details.)

14.3 Veer left at the fork, staying on the TRT.

15.3 Veer right at the bottom of the downhill, and follow the river upstream.

15.4 Turn left onto the gravel road and right again before the river. Ride past the gate, and continue along the river. The trail soon becomes paved.

15.6 Turn right on the other side of the gate onto the paved bike path.

15.8 Veer right at the fork, and follow the West Lake Bike Path along CA 89 back to the start.

17.2 Follow the BIKE ROUTE sign and turn left onto Sequoia Avenue. This takes you down near the lake and past a private beach. The bike path resumes at William Kent Beach.

17.8 Arrive back at the corner of Pineland Drive.

7 North Tahoe City Loop

There is no simple route through the maze of trails above Tahoe City. The locals have their personal favorite way up to Watson Lake and beyond. The higher you go on the mountain, the more technical and strenuous the terrain. It's a bit dodgy to map a route through here, since few of the trails are signed. Moreover, this area is a work in progress. The collective of land managers are working on a master plan that may be years in coming. Meanwhile, some of the roads and trails are beginning to change. Yet this area is too beautiful and the singletrack too fine to leave out. This loop will acquaint you with the terrain. Arm yourself with a good sense of direction, adventure, and humor. Every junction is an option.

This loop begins in Tahoe City, hits the dirt at the trailhead for the Tahoe Cross Country ski area, traverses the upper end of Burton Creek State Park, climbs over the Tahoe Rim Trail, and descends the Western States Trail before returning along the Truckee River Bike Path. If you get lost, keep heading downhill—you will eventually get to the lake.

Start: From the intersection of California Highways 89 and 28 in Tahoe City
Distance: 15.9-mile loop
Approximate riding time: 2 hours
Difficulty rating: Moderate—rocks, switchbacks, and climbing
Trail surface: 41 percent paved bike path, 28 percent singletrack, 20 percent dirt road, and 11 percent paved road
Seasons: June through October
Other trail users: Cars, hikers, and horses; no dogs allowed on singletrack in Burton Creek State Park
Land status: Lake Tahoe Basin Management Unit; California State Parks; California Tahoe Conservancy
Nearest town: Tahoe City, California
Fees and permits: No fees or permits required

Schedule: Daylight hours only in Burton Creek State Park
Maps: Maptech CD: California, High Sierra/Tahoe; USGS maps: Tahoe City, CA; Kings Beach, CA; Lake Tahoe Trail Map, Adventure Maps, Inc., 2005
Trail contacts: Lake Tahoe Basin Management Unit, 35 College Drive, South Lake Tahoe, CA 96150; (530) 543-2600; www.fs.fed.us/r5/ltbmu.
California State Parks, P.O. Box 266, Tahoma, CA 96142; (530) 525-7232; www.parks.ca.gov.
California Tahoe Conservancy, 1061 Third Street, South Lake Tahoe, CA 96150; (530) 542-5580; www.tahoecons.ca.gov.
Other: Tahoe Cross Country, Tahoe City, CA; (530) 583-5475; www.tahoexc.org; trailhead cross-country map; www.tahoexc.org/pages/trails.htm

Finding the trailhead: From Tahoe City, go to the junction of CA 89 and CA 28. The Truckee River Recreation and Public Access lot s a good place to park; the entrance to the parking lot is 500 yards south on CA 89. From the parking lot and information board for the Tahoe Rim Trail, ride across the footbridge and turn right onto the bike path. There are portable restrooms but no water. **Intersection GPS:** N 39 10.05, W 120 08.72

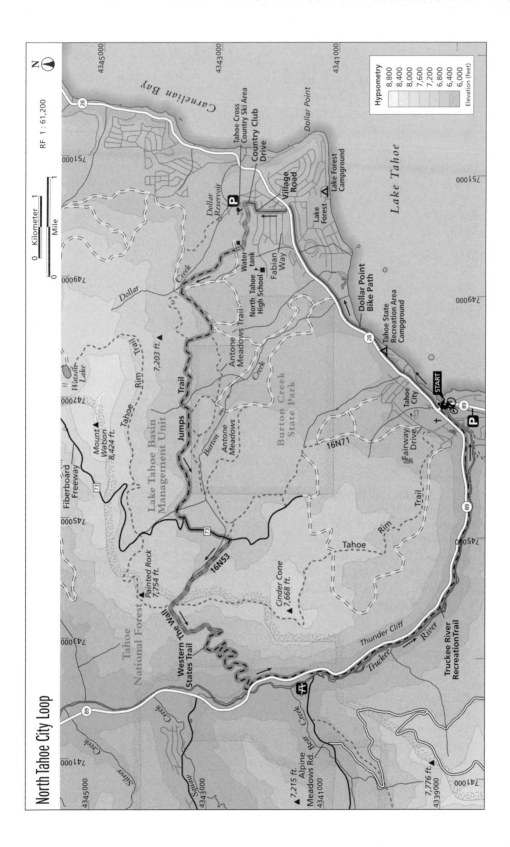

Trucking on the Truckee River Recreation Trail

Miles and Directions

0.0 **START** from the intersection of CA 89 and CA 28. Head east on CA 28 through Tahoe City. Pick up the bike path at the campground on the edge of town.

2.8 Turn left onto Fabian Way.

2.9 Turn right at Village Road.

3.2 After the road veers right at the top of the hill, turn left on Country Club Drive. In 100 yards, turn left at the EXIT sign into the parking lot for the Tahoe Cross Country ski area and ride through the parking lot.

3.3 Take the dual-track road just to the left of the information board. While there are two roads coming out of the west end of the parking lot, they will merge in 500 yards.

3.7 Turn right at the T intersection. Stay on this road straight past the water tank, ignoring all other side roads and trails.

3.9 Turn right at the fork into the woods on a smooth and level singletrack.

4.7 Arrive at a five-way intersection. Turn left on the main dirt road. Ignore the many side trails that converge through here, and focus on the main trail.

5.1 Arrive at a three-way split; turn onto the right-most trail. (**Option:** Take the middle path to Antone Meadows for a beautiful and easy ride.)

5.2 Veer right at the fork onto the dirt road.

5.5 Veer left at the fork onto the unsigned Jumps Trail. Again, try to ignore any side trails.

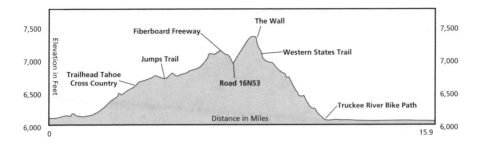

6.5 Continue straight as two narrow trails head off on the left. (**Option:** Turn left on either trail to Antone Meadows.)

7.7 Turn left onto the paved Fiberboard Freeway, Forest Service Route 73. (**Option:** If you feel like climbing, turn right and head up to the Tahoe Rim Trail. A right turn on the TRT takes you toward Watson Lake. A left turn on the TRT will take you up around Painted Rock. This will eventually drop you back down to the top of The Wall at Mile 9.0 below.)

8.2 Turn right and head up Forest Road 16N53.

9.0 Continue straight as you cross the TRT. (**Option:** Turn left on the TRT for a strenuous and technical ride into Tahoe City.)

9.2 Arrive at the top of The Wall and a steep descent.

9.5 Go left at the fork onto Western States (WS) Trail. The right is the Tevis Trail. Continue looking for the small WS Trail markers to follow down the mountain. The WS Trail is a popular equestrian trail, so watch for horses and give them a wide berth. They have the right of way.

10.0 Ignore the tempting singletrack on the right, aka the Altered States Trails.

10.1 Turn right at the T intersection where the WS Trail becomes a switchbacking singletrack.

11.2 Cross the private dirt road and continue on the singletrack.

11.4 Drop down onto the Truckee River Recreation Trail and turn left, heading under the bridge. Follow this upstream along the Truckee River back to Tahoe City.

15.9 Arrive back at the intersection of CA 89 and CA 28.

8 Antone Meadows Loop

This is the easiest way to enjoy some of the singletrack tucked in the forest above Tahoe City. The ride begins at the trailhead for the Tahoe Cross Country ski area and meanders through the heart of Burton Creek State Park. This hard-packed and level route follows the edge of the forest as it encircles Antone Meadows, never entering its sanctum. With bridges at all the creek crossings, this ride can be enjoyed early in the season when the wildflowers are at their peak. Hopefully this well-traveled course will stay intact while a master plan is drawn up for the area. Maybe signs will appear one day. Until then, have fun and explore.

Start: From the trailhead for Tahoe Cross Country ski area
Distance: 8.4-mile loop
Approximate riding time: 1 hour
Difficulty rating: Easy—well-packed trail with minor grade and obstacles
Trail surface: 73 percent singletrack and 27 percent dirt road
Seasons: June through October
Other trail users: Hikers and equestrians; no dogs allowed
Land status: Lake Tahoe Basin Management Unit; California State Parks; California Tahoe Conservancy
Nearest town: Tahoe City, California
Fees and permits: No fees or permits required
Schedule: Daylight hours only

Maps: Maptech CD: California, High Sierra/Tahoe; USGS maps: Kings Beach, CA; Tahoe City, CA; Lake Tahoe Trail Map, Adventure Maps, Inc., 2005
Trail contacts: Lake Tahoe Basin Management Unit, South Lake Tahoe, 35 College Drive, CA 96150; (530) 543-2600; www.fs.fed.us/r5/ltbmu.
California State Parks, P.O. Box 266, Tahoma, CA 96142; (530) 525-7232; www.parks.ca.gov.
California Tahoe Conservancy, 1061 Third Street, South Lake Tahoe, CA 96150; (530) 542-5580; www.tahoecons.ca.gov.
Other: Tahoe Cross Country ski area, Tahoe City, CA; (530) 583-5475; www.tahoexc.org; trailhead cross-country map: www.tahoexc.org/pages/trails.htm.

Finding the trailhead: From Tahoe City, drive 2.5 miles northeast on California Highway 28 and turn left at Fabian Way. Take the first right onto Village Road. After the road veers right at the top of the hill, turn left onto Country Club Drive. Pull into the parking lot on the left for the Highlands Community Center. The trail begins at the information board for Tahoe Cross Country ski area at the west end of the parking lot. **Trailhead GPS:** N 39 11.82, W 120 06.39

Miles and Directions

0.0 **START** from the dual track road just to the left of the information board. The second dual track that is farther to the left merges at 0.3 mile.

0.4 Turn right at the T intersection. Stay on this road straight past the water tank, ignoring all other roads and trails.

0.6 Take a right turn at the fork into the woods on a smooth and level singletrack.

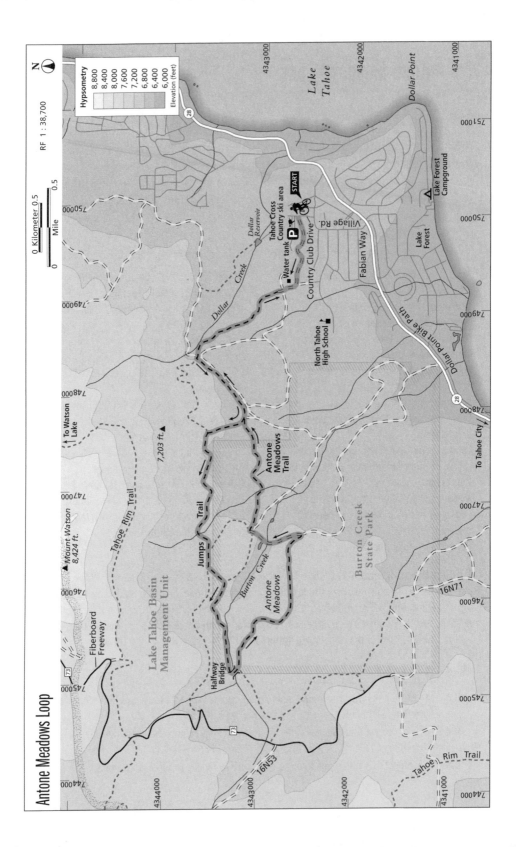

Antone Meadows Loop

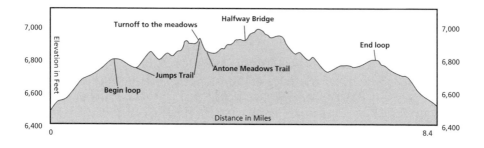

1.4 Arrive at a five-way intersection. Turn left on the main dirt road (not the wide singletrack to the left of the trail you were just on). Ignore the many side trails that converge through here, and focus on the main trail.

1.8 Arrive at a three-way split, where you will complete the loop on your return. Take the right-most trail. (**Option:** Take the middle and unsigned Antone Meadows Trail for a straight shot to the meadow.)

1.9 Veer right at the fork onto the dirt road.

2.2 Veer left at the fork onto the unsigned Jumps Trail. Again, try to ignore any side trails.

3.2 There are two trails 100 feet apart on the left that lead to Antone Meadows. Turn left at the second trail. Both paths are nice, so check out the first one the next time through.

3.4 Veer right where the trail splits, then turn right again in 50 feet onto the Antone Meadows Trail. You will pass over a couple of bridges as you encircle this little valley. The trail skirts the meadows.

4.1 Just beyond the second bridge over Burton Creek—Halfway Bridge—turn left at the fork. (**Option:** Turn right to reach the paved Forest Service Road 73—the Fiberboard Freeway.)

5.3 Turn left at the dirt road.

5.6 Shortly after the bridge over Burton Creek, you will reach a confusing intersection. Go straight on the singletrack between the boulders. In 100 feet, turn right at the NO MOTOR VEHICLES ON TRAIL sign. This is a smooth and well-tended trail, neatly lined with logs and rocks. (**FYI:** At the confusing intersection, the dirt road to the right will send you downhill. Alternatively, the trail between the posts on the left will take you back to the loop of Antone Meadows.)

6.5 This intersection completes the loop. Ride straight ahead onto the dirt road; you are now backtracking. You may notice more side trails going this direction. Stay to the left to skip them all.

7.0 Arrive back at the five-way intersection. Turn onto the second singletrack on the right, returning the way you came.

7.8 Turn left onto the dirt road and ride past the water tank on your left.

7.9 Turn left before the neighborhood.

8.4 Arrive back at the trailhead.

9 North Lake Tahoe Regional Park

The kids who live in this neighborhood are lucky. This is a park where bears show up in the outfield and squirrels steal baseballs. Moreover, there are more than 8 miles of trails packed in this 125-acre park. Some trails follow the contours, while others climb 300 feet to the park's North Ridge Trail—the highest trail in the park. Rather than follow a mapped route, be guided by your sense of adventure. Maps are posted at intersections of dirt roads that become groomed trails for cross-country skiing in the winter. Difficulty ratings are even posted to help you decide which route to take. Unsigned singletrack paths are interspersed throughout the park—nice. Several trails extend into the adjoining USDA Forest Service land. A 1.2-mile paved bike path weaves through the lower east end of the park and connects to California Highway 267. Better yet is the trail north to Regency Way and striking distance to the Tahoe Rim Trial at Brockway Summit.

Start: From anywhere in the park
Distance: As much as you want
Approximate riding time: Until you have had enough
Difficulty rating: Easy to moderate—wide trails for beginners, short but sweet singletrack; stronger riders can ride the upper trails, repeat loops, or connect to trails outside the park
Trail surface: Dirt roads, singletrack, and paved bike paths
Seasons: May through November
Other trail users: Hikers

Land status: North Tahoe Public Utility District with access to USDA Forest Service land
Nearest town: Tahoe Vista, California
Fees and permits: $3.00 parking fee
Schedule: Open daily 6:00 A.M. to 10:00 P.M.
Maps: Maptech CD: California High Sierra/Tahoe; USGS maps: Kings Beach, CA; Martis Peak, CA; North Tahoe Parks Department, Explorers Guide, North Tahoe Public Utility District
Trail contact: North Lake Tahoe Regional Park, P.O. Box 139, Tahoe Vista, CA 96148; (530) 546-5043; www.ntpud.org

Finding the trailhead: From Tahoe Vista, take National Avenue north from California Highway 28. This becomes Gun Club Road. Turn left onto Donner Road. The park is at the end of the road. **Trailhead GPS:** N 39 14.92, W 120 03.15

Miles and Directions

0.0 **START** from the west end of the paved bike path above the soccer field and ride east.

0.3 Turn left onto the singletrack and head into the woods . . .

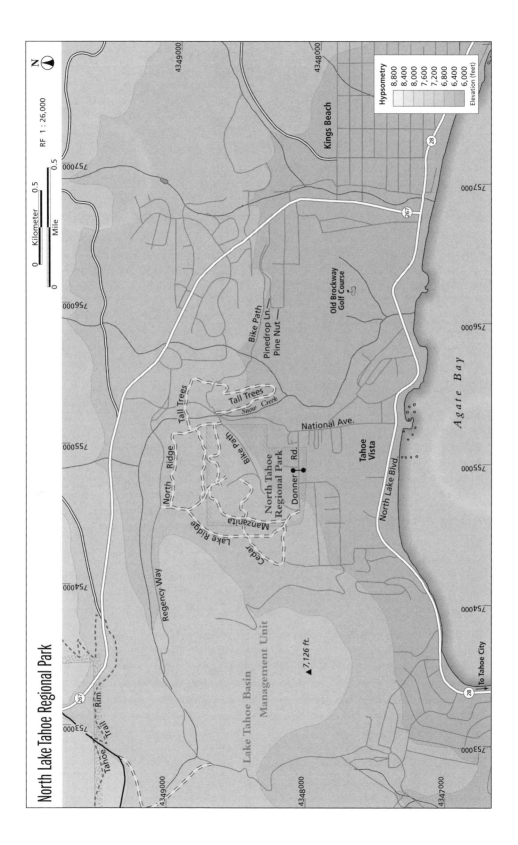

10 Brockway Summit to Tahoe City Point-to-Point

Follow the well-marked and maintained Tahoe Rim Trail (TRT) from Brockway Summit on California Highway 267 to Tahoe City. Expect about 3,000 feet of climbing and 3,900 feet of downhill—not a bad deal. The trail has just about everything, from smooth, hard-packed surface to sections of sand, loose rock, boulders, and wicked rock gardens. If you don't keep the pedals level, it's a pedal-crunching ride. Weave through mixed forests of Jeffrey pine and fir, much of which have been affected by logging. An understory of manzanita and chinquapin hug the trail, while sweeping views of Lake Tahoe and the surrounding ridges appear along the way.

An out-and-back to Watson Lake is a popular option and saves shuttling between trailheads. There are plenty of unsigned trails branching off the TRT. If you veer off course, keep heading downhill and you will eventually reach Lake Tahoe. Most of this route can be ridden in either direction, except the last 4 miles above Tahoe City. This section is steep and extremely rocky—not a pleasant uphill ride. For many riders, it's too ragged to ride down—happily. Not to worry; there are alternate ways off the mountain.

Start: From the Brockway Summit trailhead to the Tahoe Rim Trail

Distance: 18.7-mile point-to-point

Approximate riding time: 3½ to 4½ hours

Difficulty rating: Difficult—strenuous for distance, climbing, and extreme rock garden above Tahoe City

Trail surface: Singletrack

Seasons: June through October

Other trail users: Hikers and equestrians

Land status: Lake Tahoe Basin Management Unit

Nearest town: King's Beach, California

Fees and permits: No fees or permits required

Schedule: 24 hours a day

Maps: Maptech CD: California, High Sierra/Tahoe; USGS maps: Martis Peak, CA; Kings Beach, CA; Tahoe City, CA; Tahoe Rim Trail, Tahoe City to Brockway Summit Segment

Trail contacts: Lake Tahoe Basin Management Unit, USDA Forest Service, 35 College Drive, South Lake Tahoe, CA 96150; (530) 543-2600; www.fs.fed.us/r5/ltbmu. Tahoe Rim Trail Association, 948 Incline Way, Incline Village, NV 89451; (775) 298-0012; www.tahoerimtrail.org.

Finding the trailhead: From Kings Beach, take CA 267 from its intersection with California Highway 28, and drive nearly 2.7 miles toward Brockway Summit. There's a narrow parking pull-out on the left, a half mile before the summit. The trail begins just below the parking area. Maps are ususally available at the TRT kiosk. There is no water or restroom here. Be sure to pack a spare tube and patch kit for this ride—the volcanic rocks at the end are relentless. (**Note:** If you plant a car in Tahoe City for the end of the ride, be sure to take your keys with you.) **Trailhead GPS:** N 39 15.51, W 120 03.87

Scanning the horizon for the next challenge

Miles and Directions

0.0 **START** on the unsigned trail dropping down from the parking area to the information board for the Tahoe Rim Trail (TRT). The trail is easy to follow; watch for the small blue signs designating the route. Sometimes this means looking 10 feet up a tree to find the signs. Unless cued otherwise, stay on the main trail, ignoring all spur trails. You will also traverse several old roads that are being restored to a natural state; ignore them as well.

0.7 This is the first of several crossings of the paved Forest Service Route 73, aka the Fiberboard Freeway. The TRT trail is marked clearly on the other side. Each crossing can be a bailout to Tahoe City or return to Brockway Summit. This time, prepare for some climbing.

1.2 Cross an unsigned dirt road and watch for traffic up ahead at the drop-off for the next crossing of FSR 73.

1.9 Go across the paved road and head downhill through the rocks.

3.8 Pass over the first of two unsigned dirt roads. After the second road, it's a steady climb.

5.0 Cross another dirt road. The trail levels off a bit up ahead and passes through a meadow, where the trail becomes technical and rocky.

6.1 Turn left at the fork to Watson Lake.

6.3 When you see the lake, head clockwise around it. It is likely you will see more people here; the road you've been crossing leads to the lake. This is also a popular destination for hikers and bikers coming up from Tahoe City. This can be a good spot for lunch and a swim, although if the mosquitoes don't get you, the leeches might.

Brockway Summit to Tahoe City Point-to-Point

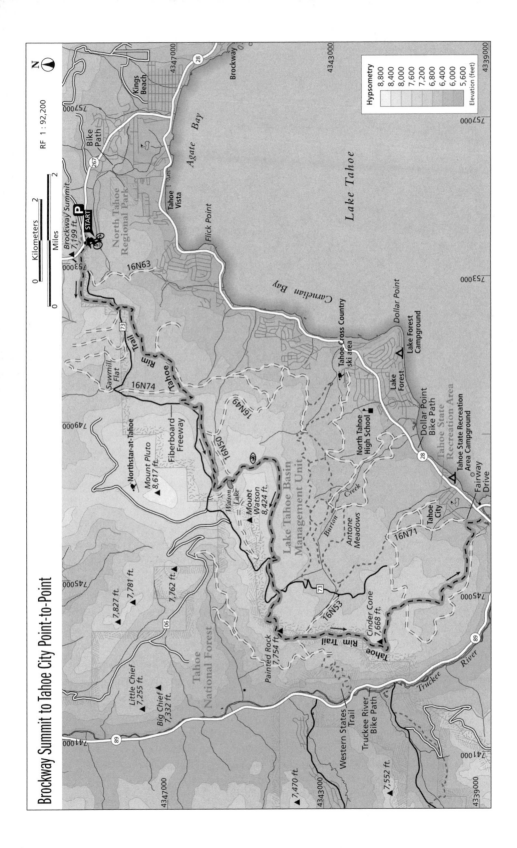

Stop but don't quit at Watson Lake

6.5 Just after crossing the stream outlet to the lake, the TRT veers left at a fork. About 120 yards up ahead, you come to a dirt road. Turn left for a short ride along the road.

6.7 Watch for the trail sign, and turn right onto the singletrack.

7.3 Veer left at the fork. (**Side trip:** Turn right and head to the top of Mount Watson.)

7.4 Photo opportunity: Enjoy one of the best views of Lake Tahoe and Twin Peaks. From here, the trail becomes loose, rocky, and steep. Watch for uphill traffic.

8.5 Turn right at the T intersection, and follow the contours of the mountain through the thick ceanothus. (**Option:** Turn left and head down the mountain.)

9.9 The trail bends right and widens. In less than 100 yards, make a left turn onto the narrower singletrack.

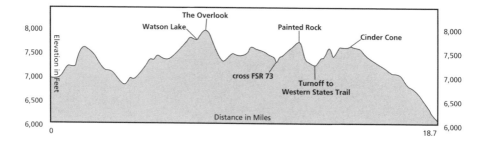

10.8 Once again cross FSR 73.

11.5 Stay to the left as you pass a couple of short spur trails on the right heading to a vista point.

11.9 Arrive at the top of Painted Rock with, yes, another great view of the lake. Check your speed on the downhill; there are several unexpected hairpin turns ahead.

12.7 Continue straight at the fork to stay on the Tahoe Rim Trail, but be advised that the TRT gets seriously rocky on the last stretch to Tahoe City. (**Option:** The most pleasant way down is to turn right. You will come to a dirt road shortly; turn right and head down to the Western States Trail. Once at the bottom, take the paved Truckee River Recreation Trail back to Tahoe City.)

12.8 Turn left onto the road for about 100 feet and then right onto the singletrack.

13.4 Veer left at the fork.

13.8 Cross the dirt road with the UNDERGROUND CABLE WARNING sign. Look up for the TRT marker at the singletrack. The trail will soon become extremely loose and rocky.

14.4 Although you reach the top of Cinder Cone, there is no respite as you cross the interminable volcanic rubble. Some say this sounds like wind chimes under your tires, others say gold coins; depends on your point of view.

15.9 Cross the dirt road.

17.9 Cross yet another dirt road to continue the steep descent. The trail narrows through the brush.

18.5 Arrive at the end of the trail; turn right onto Fairway Drive.

18.7 Arrive at California Highway 89, just west of its intersection with CA 28 in Tahoe City. You're on your own to find your car or ride.

11 Brockway Summit to Mount Baldy Out-and-Back

This quiet ride on the Tahoe Rim Trail (TRT) offers some of the best overlooks of the Lake Tahoe Basin, as well as northern views of Castle Peak, Donner Lake, and Boca Reservoir. There is no hedging that this is a steady and unrelenting climb, but it is worth the effort. For the most part, the trail is smooth and well packed. However, there is a major rock garden before the 4.0-mile mark and rocky terrain for the last mile before the turnaround. The trail skirts the top of Mount Baldy before abruptly signaling the end of the road for bikers. Bicycles are not allowed in the Mount Rose Wilderness. For another sweeping view, take the side trip to Martis Peak lookout.

Start: From the Brockway Summit trailhead to the Tahoe Rim Trail on the east side of California Highway 276

Distance: 14.5-mile out-and-back

Approximate riding time: 3 hours

Difficulty rating: Difficult—strenuous and technical

Trail surface: 90 percent singletrack and 10 percent connecting dirt roads you won't even remember

Seasons: July through October, earlier on the lower trail

Other trail users: Hikers and equestrians

Land status: Lake Tahoe Basin Management Unit

Nearest town: Kings Beach, California

Fees and permits: No fees or permits required

Schedule: 24 hours a day

Maps: Maptech CD: Nevada, Carson City/Reno/Pyramid; USGS maps: Martis Peak, NV; Tahoe Rim Trail, Brockway Summit to Mount Rose Summit Segment; Lake Tahoe Trail Map, Adventure Maps, Inc., 2005

Trail contacts: Lake Tahoe Basin Management Unit, USDA Forest Service, 35 College Drive, South Lake Tahoe, CA 96150; (530) 543-2600; www.fs.fed.us/r5/ltbmu. Tahoe Rim Trail Association, 948 Incline Way, Incline Village, NV 89451; (775) 298-0012; www.tahoerimtrail.org.

Finding the trailhead: From Kings Beach, take CA 267 from its intersection with California Highway 28 and drive 2.7 miles toward Brockway Summit. Turn right (east) at the sign for hikers and head up the dirt road—Forest Road 16N56. This is 0.5 mile before the summit and across the highway from a parking pullout on the left (west). The trailhead and parking area are just up the rise. Maps are usually available at the TRT kioski. **Trailhead GPS:** N 39 15.53, W 120 03.82

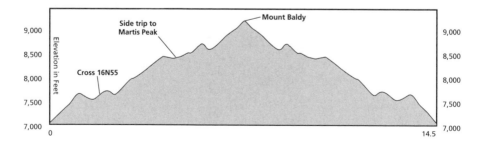

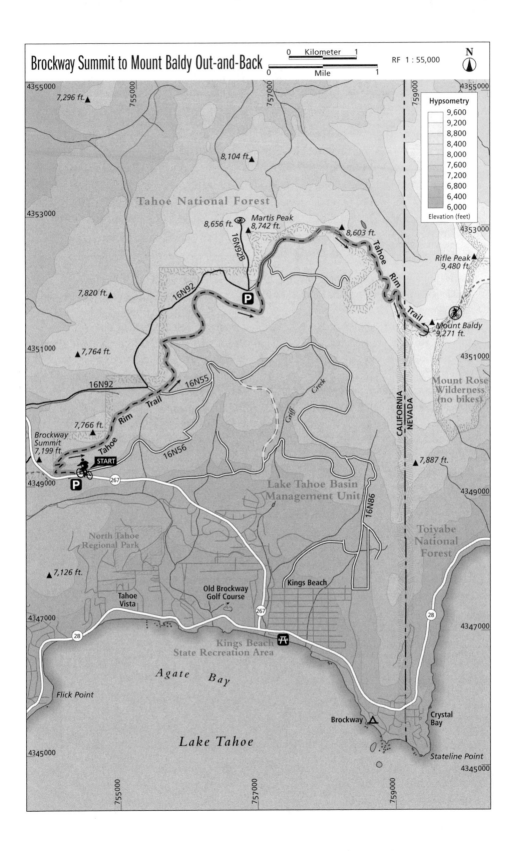

Brockway Summit to Mount Baldy Out-and-Back

0   Kilometer   1
0   Mile   1

RF 1 : 55,000

N

Hypsometry

Elevation (feet)
9,600
9,200
8,800
8,400
8,000
7,600
7,200
6,800
6,400
6,000

4355000

7,296 ft. ▲

8,104 ft. ▲

Tahoe National Forest

8,656 ft. ▲   Martis Peak
8,742 ft.

8,603 ft. ▲

Rifle Peak
9,480 ft. ▲

4353000

16N92B

16N92

7,820 ft. ▲

P

Tahoe Rim Trail

Mount Baldy
9,271 ft. ▲

4351000

▲ 7,764 ft.

16N92   16N55

Griff Creek

Tahoe   Rim   Trail

Mount Rose
Wilderness
(no bikes)

7,766 ft. ▲

16N56

CALIFORNIA
NEVADA

▲ 7,887 ft.

Brockway
Summit
7,199 ft. ▲

START

P   267

Lake Tahoe Basin
Management Unit

16N86

Toiyabe
National
Forest

4349000

North Tahoe
Regional Park

▲ 7,126 ft.

Tahoe
Vista

Old Brockway
Golf Course

Kings Beach

28

4347000

28   267

Kings Beach
State Recreation Area

Agate   Bay

Flick Point

Brockway ⌂

Crystal
Bay

Lake Tahoe

Stateline Point

4345000

755000   757000   759000

Ever-present views of the lake

Miles and Directions

0.0 **START** climbing at the trailhead for the singletrack Tahoe Rim Trail. (**Option:** For a more gradual but slightly longer climb, start on FR 16N56 at the end of the parking area. At 2.0 miles, make a sharp left onto another Forest Service road. After 0.6 mile, turn right on the Tahoe Rim Trail, picking up at Mile 1.7 below.)

1.2 Continue straight at the intersection signed SPUR TRAIL VIEW uphill to the left. As you continue on the TRT, you will pass several fading roads and spur trails; simply ignore them. (**FYI:** This spur trail takes you 0.3 mile to an outcropping of rocks.)

1.7 Cross the dirt road—Forest Road 16N33 (referred to as Forest Road 16N55 on some maps). (**FYI:** The paved Martis Peak Road—Forest Road 16N92—is about 150 yards to the left.)

2.3 At the bottom of the descent, continue straight, ignoring the spur trail on the left.

3.7 Meet the rock garden and sweeping views—the yin and yang of Tahoe. Looking south you can see Jobs Sister and Freel Peak among the profile of peaks encircling the lake.

4.0 Veer right at the slight fork at the end of the meadow.

4.1 Arrive at a T intersection with the dirt road. Turn right, following the TRT sign. (**Side trip:** For a 1.6-mile out-and-back, turn left at the dirt road and then right at the pavement. This goes to the lookout on Martis Peak (8,656 feet), with a full panoramic view of Lake Tahoe, Truckee, Verdi Peak, and the Mount Rose Wilderness.)

End of the road for bikes

4.4 Veer left at the fork in the road. Ignore the ORV trail on the right along the way.

4.6 Turn right onto the signed singletrack TRT.

5.8 The TRT turns left and climbs up the dirt road.

6.0 Continue straight onto the singletrack as the road veers to the right.

6.9 Check out the craggy overlook and must-see view on the right.

7.3 The trail ends midstride for bikes. Please don't think of poaching this one. This is federal wilderness, and bikes aren't welcome. Retrace your way back down the mountain.

14.5 Arrive back at the trailhead.

12 Tyrolean Point-to-Point

Warm up through Tahoe Meadows on the Tahoe Rim Trail (TRT) before peeling off on an 1,800-feet drop near the base of Diamond Peak ski resort. Like a river, this route is fed by several tributary paths; they merge halfway down the mountain. At the convergence, the Tyrolean Trail gets steeper and rockier, with some sandy sections. By the end of the season, parts of the trail are a powdery dust. This is not a dedicated downhill run—so watch for hikers and check the speed, particularly on the lower half of the trail. The maze of trails on the upper slope offers alternate access on odd-numbered days, when bikes are not allowed on the TRT. This can be ridden as a loop, with a ride back up the highway.

Start: From the Tahoe Meadows trailhead to the Tahoe Rim Trail

Distance: 5.9-mile point-to-point

Approximate riding time: 45 minutes to 1 hour

Difficulty rating: Difficult—steep and rocky descent

Trail surface: Singletrack

Seasons: Mid-June through October

Other trail users: Hikers

Land status: Lake Tahoe Basin Management Unit

Nearest town: Incline Village, Nevada

Fees and permits: No fees or permits required

Schedule: Ride the Tahoe Rim Trail from Mount Rose to Tunnel Creek Road on *even-numbered days only.*

Maps: Maptech CD: Nevada, Carson City/Reno/Pyramid; USGS map: Mount Rose, NV; Lake Tahoe Trail Map, Adventure Maps, Inc., 2005

Trail contact: Lake Tahoe Basin Management Unit, USDA Forest Service, 35 College Drive, South Lake Tahoe, CA 96150; (530) 543-2600; www.fs.fed.us/r5/ltbmu

Finding the trailhead: From Incline Village, drive north on Nevada Highway 431 (Mount Rose Highway) to the Tahoe Meadows parking area on the right; this is 7.2 miles from its intersection with Nevada Highway 28. There are restrooms but no water. **Trailhead GPS:** N 39 18.45, W 119 54.47

Miles and Directions

0.0 **START** from the Tahoe Meadows trailhead on the Mount Rose Highway. The ride begins through Tahoe Meadows, crossing Ophir Creek along the way.

0.7 Turn left at the T intersection.

0.9 Veer right at the fork with the Ophir Creek Trail. (**FYI:** In case you are wondering, a left turn offers a great overlook of the Carson Valley in 2.3 miles and a technical 7.0-mile descent to Davis Creek County Park on the Old Interstate 395. However, a sign is posted near the Ophir Creek Trailhead: NOT RECOMMENDED FOR MOUNTAIN BIKES.)

1.7 You will leave the Tahoe Rim Trail where the trail levels off. Take the middle path between the TRT on the left and a path on the right to an overlook next to the boulders.

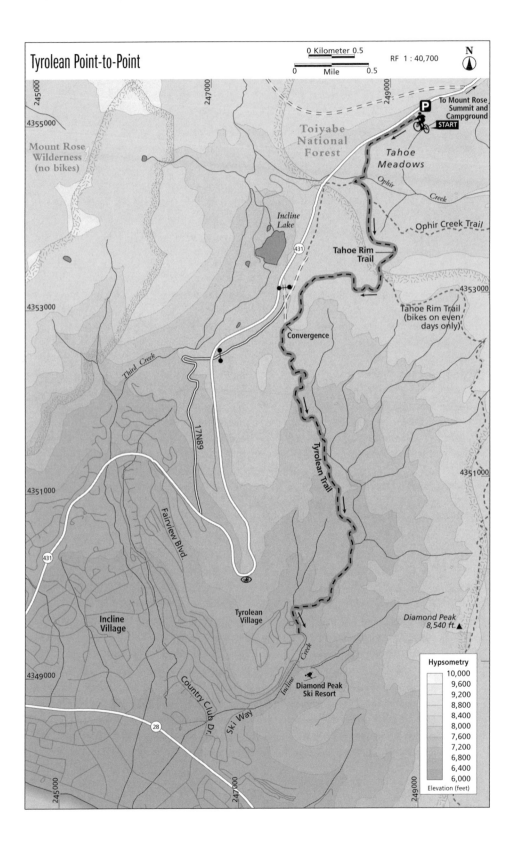

Tyrolean Point-to-Point

0 Kilometer 0.5

0 Mile 0.5

RF 1 : 40,700

N

To Mount Rose
Summit and
Campground

START

Toiyabe
National
Forest

Tahoe
Meadows

Mount Rose
Wilderness
(no bikes)

Ophir Creek

Ophir Creek Trail

Incline
Lake

431

Tahoe Rim
Trail

Tahoe Rim Trail
(bikes on even
days only)

Convergence

Third Creek

17N89

Tyrolean Trail

Fairview Blvd.

431

Diamond Peak
8,540 ft.

Incline
Village

Tyrolean
Village

Incline Creek

Country Club Dr.

Diamond Peak
Ski Resort

Ski Way

28

Hypsometry

10,000
9,600
9,200
8,800
8,400
8,000
7,600
7,200
6,800
6,400
6,000

Elevation (feet)

Heading out from Tahoe Meadows

2.0 The trail widens into a dirt road. There will be several trails converging as you descend. Have fun—there is more than one path through the upper woods.

2.3 Veer left at the fork. When in doubt about which way to go as side trails merge, follow the bike tracks.

2.4 Veer left at the fork.

2.9 Veer left onto the singletrack through the USDA Forest Service markers: BE RESPONSIBLE. This is the convergence point and heart of the ride. (**Note:** Before the markers, a trail merges from the right—this trail feeds from the highway and several alternate routes.)

3.9 Veer left at the fork. (**FYI:** A right turn takes you out to the highway.)

4.0 Cross the creek on the bridge, and turn right at the fork on the other side. Follow the creek downstream.

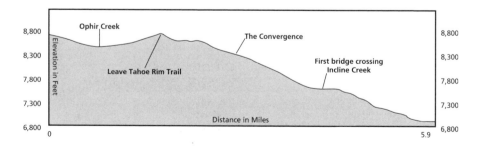

4.6 Veer left and downhill at the fork.

5.7 Turn left immediately after crossing the bridge, and follow the creek along the edge of the neighborhood.

5.9 The ride ends at the chain across the trail. Turn left on the pavement to head into town. (**Loop option:** It's a 7.5-mile ride back to the Tahoe Meadows trailhead. To get there, turn left and ride through the parking lot of Diamond Peak Ski Resort. Turn right onto Fairview Boulevard, and follow this to NV 431. Make a right turn and head back up to your vehicle. There is a bike lane up the highway.)

Alternate trailhead: From Incline Village, drive 6.3 miles north on NV 431 from the intersection of NV 28. There is a small pullout at a Forest Service gate. **Trailhead GPS:** N 39 17.90, W 119 55.26

Start at the gate and ride down the old highway—Forest Road 17N89. Veer left at the first junction in 0.8 mile onto a parallel singletrack. Veer left again at the next fork and you should come to the convergence—just over a mile from the start. Veer right through the Forest Service markers onto the singletrack.

13 Tahoe Meadows to Marlette Lake to Flume Trail Point-to-Point

Brilliant singletrack, spectacular views, and commercial shuttles make this the most popular bike route along the Tahoe Rim Trail (TRT). Riding here is nearly a social event. To limit congestion and keep other trail users happy, bike this segment of the TRT on even-numbered days only. Ride through thin alpine forests and maneuver around granite boulders on hard-packed trail with some serious sandy sections. The views move back and forth between the verdant Tahoe Basin on the west and the contrasting Washoe Valley to the east. The overall grade to Tunnel Creek Road is undulating and gradual, strewn with rocky step-ups and drops. After crossing Tunnel Creek Road, the climb is unrelenting to the high point near the Marlette Overlook. From there, it is mostly downhill or level until the end. While the Flume Trail is one of the flattest trails in Tahoe, it is narrow, with some serious drop-offs. The Tunnel Creek Road is steep, wide, and sandy—a good reason not to start from this end. For a more moderate journey, ride from Tahoe Meadows directly to the Flume Trail and end up at Spooner Lake.

Start: From the Tahoe Meadows trailhead to the Tahoe Rim Trail
Distance: 23.7-mile point-to-point
Approximate riding time: 3 to 4 hours
Difficulty rating: Difficult—long, strenuous, and technical
Trail surface: 76 percent singletrack and 24 percent dirt road
Seasons: Mid-June through October
Other trail users: Hikers and equestrians

The drop-dead-gorgeous view

Land status: Lake Tahoe Basin Management Unit; Lake Tahoe–Nevada State Park

Nearest town: Incline Village, Nevada

Fees and permits: $2.00 per rider backcountry fee collected at Spooner Lake

Schedule: Ride the Tahoe Rim Trail from Mount Rose to Tunnel Creek Road on *even-numbered days only*

Maps: Maptech CD: Nevada, Carson City/Reno/Pyramid; USGS maps: Mount Rose, NV; Marlette Lake, NV; Tahoe Rim Trail, Tahoe Meadows to Spooner Summit Segment; Lake Tahoe Trail Map, Adventure Maps, Inc., 2005

Trail contacts: Lake Tahoe Basin Management Unit, USDA Forest Service, 35 College Drive, South Lake Tahoe, CA 96150; (530) 543-2600; www.fs.fed.us/r5/ltbmu. Lake Tahoe–Nevada State Park, P.O. Box 8867, Incline Village, NV 89452; (775) 831-0494; http://parks.nv.gov/lt.htm. Tahoe Rim Trail Association, 948 Incline Way, Incline Village, NV 89451; (775) 298-0012; www.tahoerimtrail.org.

Commercial shuttle service: Flume Trail Mountain Bike; (775) 749-5349; www.the flumetrail.com; check the Web cam for weather.

Finding the trailhead: From Incline Village, drive north on Nevada Highway 431 (Mount Rose Highway) to the Tahoe Meadows parking area on the right; this is 7.2 miles from its intersection with Nevada Highway 28. Maps are usually available at the TRT kiosk. There are restrooms but no water. **Trailhead GPS:** N 39 18.45, W 119 54.47

Shuttle: There is no parking where the trail ends on NV 28 across from Hidden Beach. The best place to drop a car is in Incline Village. At the end of the ride, take the trail option to Ponderosa Ranch Road.

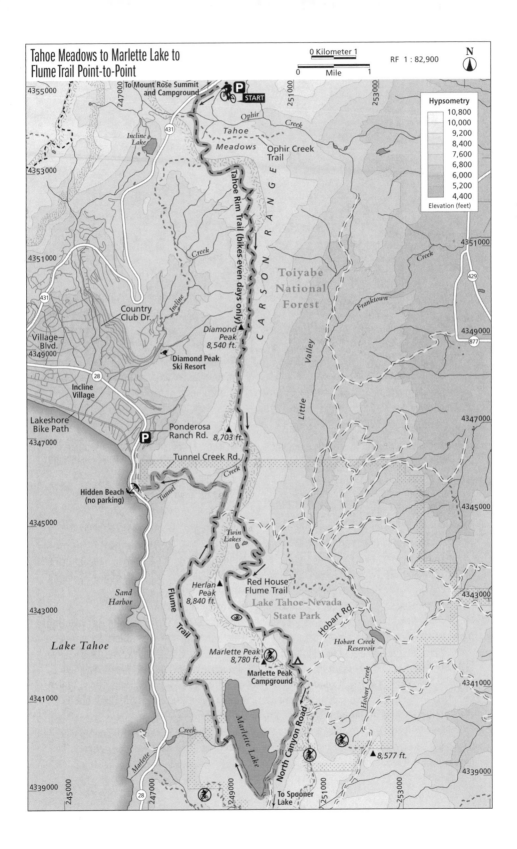

Tahoe Meadows to Marlette Lake to Flume Trail Point-to-Point

RF 1 : 82,900

0 Kilometer 1

0 Mile 1

N

Hypsometry

10,800
10,000
9,200
8,400
7,600
6,800
6,000
5,200
4,400

Elevation (feet)

4355000

247000

To Mount Rose Summit and Campground

START

Ophir Creek

4353000

Tahoe Meadows

Ophir Creek Trail

Incline Lake

431

Tahoe Rim Trail (bikes even days only)

CARSON RANGE

251000

253000

Toiyabe National Forest

4351000

Creek

Franktown

429

Creek

Country Club Dr.

Incline Creek

Diamond Peak 8,540 ft.

Little Valley

4349000

Village Blvd.

4349000

Diamond Peak Ski Resort

877

28

Incline Village

Lakeshore Bike Path

4347000

P

Ponderosa Ranch Rd.

8,703 ft.

4347000

Tunnel Creek Rd.

Creek

Hidden Beach (no parking)

Tunnel

4345000

4345000

Twin Lakes

Flume Trail

Herlan Peak 8,840 ft.

Red House Flume Trail

Lake Tahoe-Nevada State Park

Hobart Rd.

4343000

4343000

Sand Harbor

Marlette Peak 8,780 ft.

Hobart Creek Reservoir

Hobart Creek

Lake Tahoe

Marlette Peak Campground

4341000

4341000

North Canyon Road

Marlette Lake

8,577 ft.

4339000

Creek

4339000

245000

Marlette

247000

249000

28

To Spooner Lake

251000

253000

Miles and Directions

0.0 **START** from the Tahoe Meadows trailhead, Mount Rose Highway. The ride begins through Tahoe Meadows, crossing several rivulets along the way. You will follow the well-signed TRT for the next 13.7 miles.

0.6 Cross Ophir Creek.

0.7 Turn left at the T intersection.

0.9 Veer right at the fork with the Ophir Creek Trail. (**FYI:** A left turn offers a great overlook of the Carson Valley in 2.3 miles and a technical 7.0-mile descent to Davis Creek County Park on the Old Interstate 395. However, a sign is posted near the Ophir Creek trailhead: NOT RECOMMENDED FOR MOUNTAIN BIKES.)

1.7 Veer left where the trail levels off and there is an overlook on the right.

4.3 Washoe Valley comes into view to the east.

6.0 You have just ridden around Diamond Peak; pull over through here to absorb the view from one of the rocky outcroppings. Incline Village and the Diamond Peak Ski Resort are below.

8.5 Arrive at the intersection of Tunnel Creek Road and several options. For this route, continue straight on the Tahoe Rim Trail. Brace yourself for a steep climb toward Herlan Peak. (**Option 1:** Turn left and drop down to the Red House Flume Trail for a long climb up Hobart Road to Marlette Lake. **Option 2:** Turn right to the northern end of the Flume Trail. From here you can ride the Flume Trail south to Marlette Lake, up over the hill on the North Canyon Road, and end at Spooner Lake. **Option 3:** Turn right and ride Tunnel Creek Road to Hidden Beach on NV 28.)

8.8 Early in the season you will arrive at one of the shallow Twin Lakes. By summer's end, things are less obvious. Stay to the left of the multiuser trail sign. The climb begins up ahead.

11.4 Continue straight at the junction to the Sand Harbor Overlook. You have nearly reached the highest point on the ride. (**Side trip:** The view from the granite cliff on this 1.2-mile loop is drop-dead gorgeous. However, any bikes on this trail must be walked, carried, or stashed.)

12.1 Turn right for a short out-and-back to the overlook of Marlette Lake before starting downhill. (**Option:** Skip the lookout and shave 0.15 mile off the rest of the mileage cues.)

12.5 Veer left on the bike route toward Marlette Peak Campground. The two trails will merge on the other side of the campground.

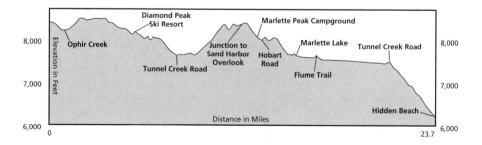

13.2 Continue past the campground sign pointing left. (**FYI:** That's a pit toilet on the left.)

13.7 Arrive at the junction with Hobart Road. Ride straight onto the dirt road, following the signs to Marlette Lake and Spooner Lake. You are now leaving the Tahoe Rim Trail, which continues on a no-bike trail to Snow Valley Peak.

14.1 Pause for the striking view and illusion of Marlette Lake flowing directly into Lake Tahoe.

15.4 Continue straight at the intersection, following the sign to MARLETTE LAKE DAM & FLUME TRAIL. Stay on the dirt road heading clockwise around the lake. (**Option:** Turn left if you want to finish the ride at Spooner Lake.)

16.7 Ride along the edge of the lake to reach the trailhead to the Flume Trail. Early in the season, this may mean riding through some water near the dam. The Flume Trail itself starts out a little ragged but soon smoothes out for a flat and narrow ride along the edge of the hillside. Sections of the trail are subject to slides and must be walked. Watch out for the granite boulders that line the trail; hitting a handlebar against these can send you into space.

21.0 This is the end of the Flume Trail. Ride straight downhill on the wide Tunnel Creek Road; ignore all the side trails along the way. Be prepared for the sand pits. (**Short side trip:** Before heading down Tunnel Creek Road, turn left onto one of the spur trails for a last overlook of Lake Tahoe.) (**Option:** For a return loop to the Tahoe Meadows trailhead, turn right and climb back up to the Tahoe Rim Trail.)

23.0 Ignore the trail on the right.

23.5 Turn left sharply toward Hidden Beach. (**Option:** Turn right onto Tunnel Creek Road to Ponderosa Ranch Road. This will take you to NV 28 in Incline Village. If you are riding back up to Tahoe Meadows, this is the way to go.

23.7 Arrive at NV 28 and the end of the ride. If you have timed it right, shuttle service will pick you up here. (**FYI:** Hidden Beach is across the highway with a hidden sign.)

◀ *Stair-stepping on the rim*

14 Flume Trail Loop

Welcome to the most photographed trail in Tahoe—the Flume Trail. With commercial shuttle service, there are several ways to explore this area. This loop connects the famed ride overlooking Lake Tahoe with the lesser traveled Red House Flume Trail overlooking Carson City. Following abandoned flumes built to convey water from Marlette Lake, the trails are nearly flat. The challenge is getting to them. Spooner Lake is the most popular starting point and entails a 4.0-mile climb up North Canyon on a well-graded dirt road that will seem 2 miles too long. The payoff is just beyond Marlette Lake on the 4.4-mile Flume Trail—a narrow trail hugging the cliffs above Lake Tahoe's Sand Harbor. Riders with vertigo may want to skip this ride; for a moderate ride, head down Tunnel Creek Road for a shuttle back to Spooner Lake. Otherwise continue on the full and more peaceful loop. Sandy downhill sections, a dicey stream crossing, and the long climb up Hobart Road are compensated in early summer with a brilliant display of mule's ears wildflowers. In fall, vibrant stands of aspen offer their own rewards.

Start: From Spooner Lake

Distance: 22.0-mile loop, with 13.0-mile point-to-point option

Approximate riding time: 3 to 4 hours

Difficulty rating: Full loop is difficult–strenuous climbs, narrow singletrack, sandy descents, and a precarious stream crossing. The point-to-point option is moderate–long climb and precipitous singletrack

Trail surface: 30 percent singletrack and 70 percent dirt road

Seasons: June through October

Other trail users: Hikers and equestrians

Land status: Lake Tahoe-Nevada State Park

Nearest town: Incline Village, Nevada

Fees and permits: $6.00 day use fee at Spooner Lake; more for vehicles with more than four bikes

Schedule: 24 hours a day

Maps: Maptech CD: Nevada, Carson City/Reno/Pyramid; USGS maps: Glenbrook, NV; Marlette Lake, NV

Trail contact: Lake Tahoe-Nevada State Park, P.O. Box 8867, Incline Village, NV 89452; (775) 831-0494; http://parks.nv.gov/lt.htm

Commercial shuttle service: Flume Trail Mountain Bike; (775) 749-5349; www.theflumetrail.com; check Web cam for weather

Finding the trailhead: From Incline Village, take Nevada Highway 28 south about 10 miles along the east side of Lake Tahoe. The entrance to Spooner Lake is on the left.

From South Lake Tahoe; drive north about 12 miles on U.S. Highway 50 and turn left onto NV 28. The entrance to the Spooner Lake day use area is on the right 0.5 mile on NV 28. Restrooms and water are available at the trailhead. **Trailhead GPS:** N 39 06.37, W 119 54.96

Miles and Directions

0.0 START from the information board near the restrooms and follow the sign to Marlette Lake and the Flume Trail.

Be alert for slides on the Flume Trail

0.2   Follow the NORTH CANYON TRAIL sign, and stay on the North Canyon Road all the way to Marlette Lake.

2.8   Ignore the singletrack just before the outhouse. It leads to a no-bike section of the Tahoe Rim Trail.

3.8   Skip the singletrack on the right to Snow Valley Peak, and trudge on.

4.0   Reach the summit before descending to Marlette Lake. For those doing the shuttle to Tunnel Creek Road, this is the end of the climbing.

4.6   Turn left at the intersection, and follow the sign around Marlette Lake to the Flume Trail. For much of the summer, the assortment of wildflowers along here is exceptional.

4.9   After you cross a creek near the lake's shore, veer right to stay on the road. Ignore the side trails.

5.9   Depending on the water level, you may have to ride through some water or carry your bike on higher ground to reach the dam. Welcome to the Flume Trail. The initial drop is ragged as you begin following the path of the old wooden flumes and enjoying the world-famous view. Sections of the trail are subject to slides and must be walked. Watch out for the granite boulders that line the trail; hitting a handlebar against these can send you over the edge. Also bear in mind, your bike follows your gaze.

10.3   Arrive at the intersection with Tunnel Creek Road. Turn right for the steep climb toward Red House. (**Short side trip:** Turn left onto one of the spur trails for a last overlook of the lake. **Option 1:** Continue straight down Tunnel Creek Road for a shuttle back to Spooner Lake. **Option 2:** Turn around and ride the Flume Trail back to Spooner Lake.)

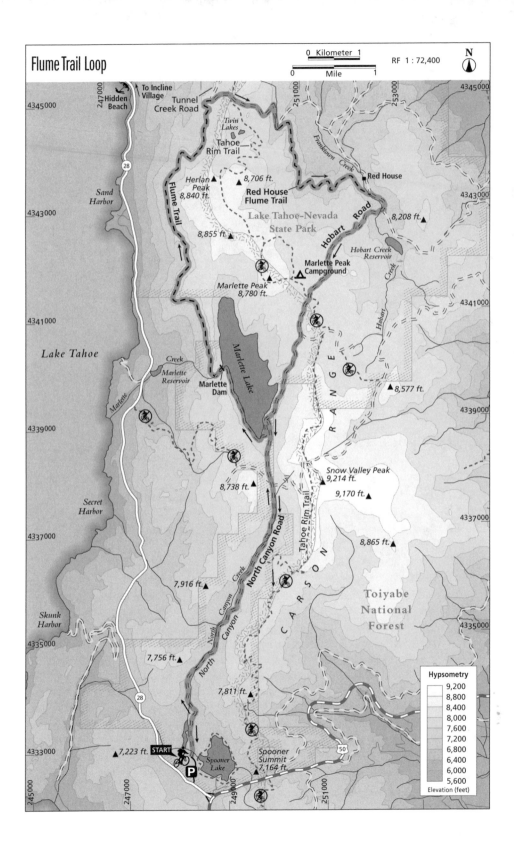

Flume Trail Loop

0 Kilometer 1

0 Mile 1

RF 1 : 72,400

N

4345000

247000

To Incline Village

Hidden Beach

Tunnel Creek Road

Twin Lakes

Tahoe Rim Trail

251000

253000

4345000

Franktown Creek

Red House

Sand Harbor

Herlan Peak 8,840 ft.

8,706 ft.

Red House Flume Trail

Lake Tahoe–Nevada State Park

Hobart Road

8,208 ft.

4343000

4343000

8,855 ft.

Hobart Creek Reservoir

Flume Trail

Marlette Peak Campground

Hobart Creek

4341000

Marlette Peak 8,780 ft.

R A N G E

4341000

Lake Tahoe

Creek

Marlette Reservoir

Marlette Lake

8,577 ft.

4339000

Marlette Dam

4339000

Marlette Creek

Snow Valley Peak 9,214 ft.

8,738 ft.

9,170 ft.

Secret Harbor

Tahoe Rim Trail

C A R S O N

8,865 ft.

4337000

4337000

7,916 ft.

North Canyon Road

Toiyabe National Forest

Skunk Harbor

North Canyon Creek

4335000

4335000

7,756 ft.

28

7,811 ft.

Hypsometry

9,200
8,800
8,400
8,000
7,600
7,200
6,800
6,400
6,000
5,600

Elevation (feet)

4333000

7,223 ft. START

Spooner Lake

Spooner Summit 7,164 ft.

50

P

245000

247000

249000

251000

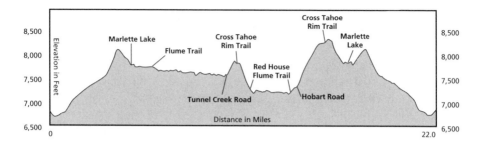

10.6 Cross the intersection with the Tahoe Rim Trail and follow the sign to Red House. (**Option:** Turn right onto the TRT for an alternate route back to Marlette Lake.)

10.8 Continue straight, passing another trail on the right to Twin Lakes. Heads up for a steep and sandy descent.

11.3 At the junction, turn right toward Red House.

11.5 Turn right at the fork to Marlette Lake and Hobart Creek Reservoir. Following the pipeline, you are now on the Red House Flume Trail. You can see Carson City through the trees.

13.4 Veer right at the fork toward Marlette Lake, still following the pipe.

13.7 The Red House Flume Trail ends as you carefully carry your bike across the dam on Franktown Creek. About 100 yards beyond the creek, make a sharp right turn up the road.

14.1 Turn right toward Marlette Lake on Hobart Road for the interminable climb up Sunflower Hill. As you climb, you can see Hobart Creek Reservoir on the left.

15.4 Veer right at the fork, following the well-traveled route.

15.8 Continue straight at the intersection with the Tahoe Rim Trail, following the road to Marlette Lake.

16.2 Pause for the striking view and illusion of Marlette Lake flowing directly into Lake Tahoe.

17.4 This completes the loop portion of the ride. Turn left for the return to Spooner Lake.

18.1 Arrive at the last summit and cruise down North Canyon Road.

21.9 Cross the trail to Spooner Lake and head up to the parking lot.

22.0 Arrive back at the trailhead.

15 Spooner Summit to South Camp Peak Out-and-Back

Head out on the Tahoe Rim Trail (TRT) for a steady climb to South Camp Peak and a stellar view of the Tahoe Basin. This northern access to the peak involves more climbing and is less technical than the assault from Kingsbury Grade. The well-marked singletrack is smooth and hard packed on the lower flanks, with increasing and loose rocks on the upper trail. You will ride in and out of a changing forest with exposed sections of low-lying manzanita, chinquapin, and sagebrush. Go all the way to Kingsbury Grade if you can arrange the shuttle, or go the distance for a full 24.4-mile out-and-back.

Start: From Spooner Summit trailhead to the Tahoe Rim Trail, U.S. Highway 50
Distance: 11.2-mile out-and-back
Approximate riding time: 2 to 3 hours
Difficulty rating: Moderate to difficult—steady climb, mostly hard packed with technical sections that are loose and rocky
Trail surface: Singletrack
Seasons: June through October
Other trail users: Hikers and equestrians
Land status: Lake Tahoe Basin Management Unit
Nearest town: Incline Village, Nevada

Fees and permits: No fees or permits required
Schedule: 24 hours a day
Maps: Maptech CD: Nevada, Carson City/Reno/Pyramid; USGS map: Glenbrook, NV; Tahoe Rim Trail, Spooner Summit—Kingsbury Segment
Trail contacts: Lake Tahoe Basin Management Unit, USDA Forest Service, 35 College Drive, South Lake Tahoe, CA 96150; (530) 543-2600; www.fs.fed.us/r5/ltbmu. Tahoe Rim Trail Association, 948 Incline Way, Incline Village, NV 89451; (775) 298-0012; www.tahoerimtrail.org.

Finding the trailhead: From Incline Village, take Nevada Highway 28 south along the east side of Lake Tahoe. Turn left at the junction with US 50. Drive 0.7 mile to the Spooner Picnic Area on the right. Maps are usually available at the TRT kiosk. There is parking and pit toilets but no water.

From South Lake Tahoe, drive north on US 50 toward Carson City. The trailhead is on the right past the summit at the Spooner Picnic Area, 0.7 mile from the junction with NV 28. **Trailhead GPS:** N 39 06.20, W 119 53.73

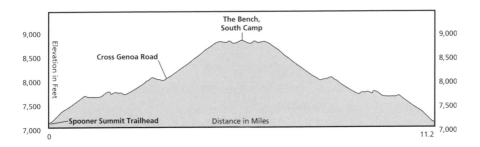

Enjoyable vistas of Lake Tahoe and beyond

Miles and Directions

0.0 **START** from the Tahoe Rim Trail information board, following the GENOA ROAD 3 MILES, RIDGETOP VIEW 5 sign. The ride begins with a stiff climb through the forest, with views of Spooner Lake and Lake Tahoe along the way.

2.2 Cross a dirt road—twice—following the well-traveled singletrack.

3.3 After a welcomed descent, you cross Genoa Road. The climbing resumes with a vengeance all the way to the summit.

4.0 New trees are emerging where the forest has been cleared of dead timber. Bark beetles invaded this area and killed many of the trees. Expect more loose rock as you climb.

5.0 At the end of the forest is the final steep pitch to the top. Once on the crest, you cruise along the South Camp plateau.

5.6 Arrive at The Bench on the right side of the trail, with views of Lake Tahoe, Heavenly ski area, Freel Peak, Emerald Bay, the Desolation Wilderness, and Granite Chief Wilderness. The trail is nearly level along the broad ridge; explore it a bit before returning the way you came. (**Option:** Continue 6.6 miles to the Kingsbury Grade trailhead for an extended out-and-back or, if you planned ahead, a shuttle pickup.)

11.2 Arrive back at the Spooner Summit trailhead.

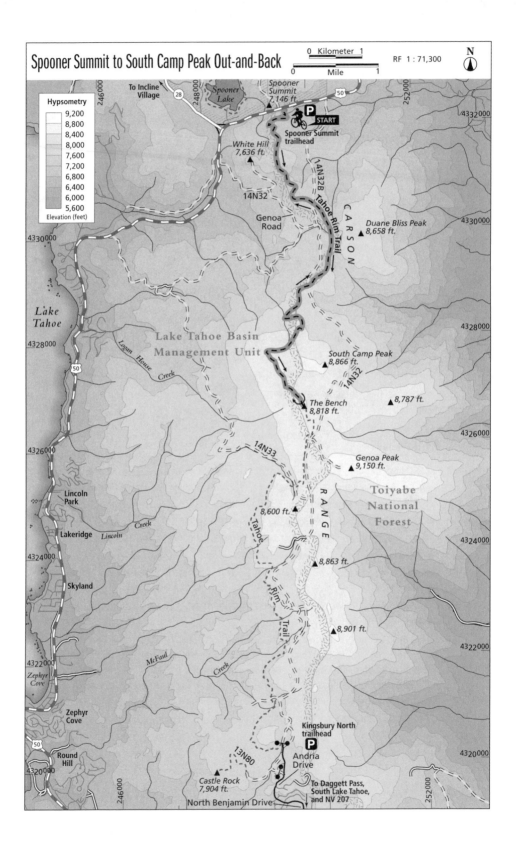

Spooner Summit to South Camp Peak Out-and-Back

0 Kilometer 1
0 Mile 1

RF 1 : 71,300

N

To Incline Village

28

Spooner Lake

Spooner Summit 7,146 ft.

50

START

Spooner Summit trailhead

White Hill 7,636 ft.

14N32B

Tahoe Rim Trail

14N32

Genoa Road

C A R S O N

Duane Bliss Peak 8,658 ft.

Lake Tahoe

Logan House Creek

Lake Tahoe Basin Management Unit

South Camp Peak 8,866 ft.

▲ 8,787 ft.

The Bench 8,818 ft.

50

14N33

Genoa Peak 9,150 ft.

Toiyabe National Forest

8,600 ft.

Lincoln Park

Lakeridge

Lincoln

Creek

Tahoe

Rim

Trail

R A N G E

▲ 8,863 ft.

Skyland

▲ 8,901 ft.

Zephyr Cove

McFaul

Creek

Zephyr Cove

Kingsbury North trailhead

50

Round Hill

13N80

Andria Drive

Castle Rock 7,904 ft.

To Daggett Pass, South Lake Tahoe, and NV 207

North Benjamin Drive

4332000
4330000
4328000
4326000
4324000
4322000
4320000

246000
248000
252000

16 Kingsbury Grade to South Camp Peak Out-and-Back

This is a beautiful trail in every sense of the word. Views of Lake Tahoe follow you as you wind through the pine forest, culminating at the high meadow along the ridge of South Camp Peak. The turnaround point is The Bench, a popular log seat in the middle of a magnificent, sweeping view of the Tahoe Basin. This section of the Tahoe Rim Trail (TRT) is on par with the view—narrow and smooth hard pack with plenty of obstacles to hold your attention. Except for the rugged first 0.5 mile, the gain in elevation is gradual and follows the contours of the mountain. Since the trailhead is readily accessible to town, expect a fair amount of traffic. You can ride the TRT all the way to Spooner Summit as a point-to-point or go the full distance as a 24.4-mile out-and-back.

Start: From Tahoe Rim Trail just north of Kingsbury Grade
Distance: 13.2-mile out-and-back
Approximate riding time: 2½ hours
Difficulty rating: Moderate to difficult—mostly hard packed with technical sections that are loose and rocky; some hike-a-bike
Trail surface: Singletrack
Seasons: June through October
Other trail users: Hikers and equestrians
Land status: Lake Tahoe Basin Management Unit
Nearest town: South Lake Tahoe, California/Stateline, Nevada

Fees and permits: No fees or permits required
Schedule: 24 hours a day
Maps: Maptech CD: Nevada, Carson City/Reno/Pyramid; Hawthorne/Yerington/Tonopah; USGS maps: Glenbrook, NV; South Lake Tahoe, CA; Tahoe Rim Trail, Spooner Summit—Kingsbury Segment
Trail contacts: Lake Tahoe Basin Management Unit, USDA Forest Service, 35 College Drive, South Lake Tahoe, CA 96150; (530) 543-2600; www.fs.fed.us/r5/ltbmu. Tahoe Rim Trail Association, 948 Incline Way, Incline Village, NV 89451; (775) 298-0012; www.tahoerimtrail.org.

Finding the trailhead: From South Lake Tahoe and Stateline, take Nevada Highway 207 (Kingsbury Grade) east 2.7 miles and turn left onto North Benjamin Drive. Follow North Benjamin Drive as it turns into Andria Drive. Continue until the pavement ends at the parking area, just before a gate to Forest Road 14N32; this is about 1.8 miles from Kingsbury Grade. Maps

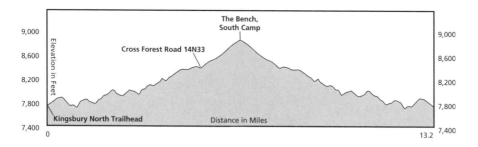

Kingsbury Grade to South Camp Peak Out-and-Back

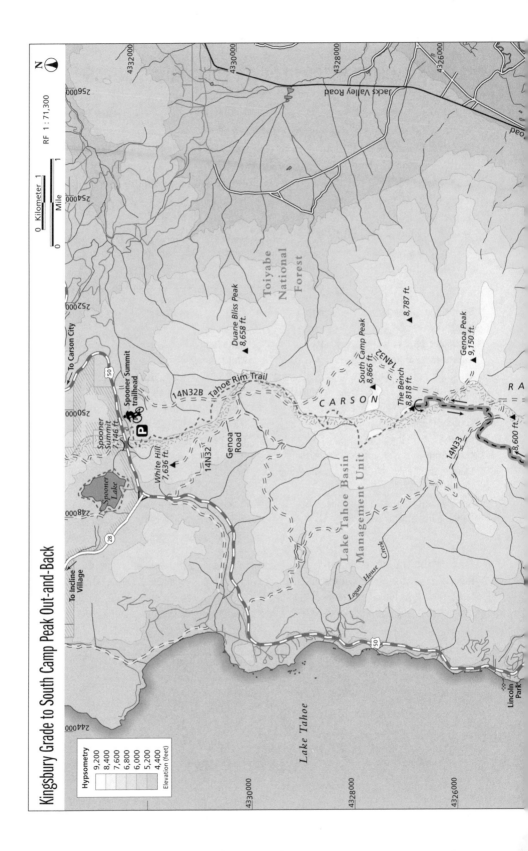

N

0 Kilometer 1

0 Mile 1

RF 1 : 71,300

Hypsometry

9,200
8,400
7,600
6,800
6,000
5,200
4,400

Elevation (feet)

Lake Tahoe

Toiyabe National Forest

CARSON

Lake Tahoe Basin Management Unit

Spooner Lake

Spooner Summit 7,146 ft.

Spooner Summit trailhead

White Hill 7,636 ft.

Duane Bliss Peak 8,658 ft.

South Camp Peak 8,866 ft.

The Bench 8,818 ft.

Genoa Peak 9,150 ft.

8,787 ft.

8,600 ft.

Tahoe Rim Trail

Genoa Road

14N32B

14N32

14N33

14N32

To Carson City

To Incline Village

Jacks Valley Road

Logan House Creek

Lincoln Park

R A N G E

peo

The view from South Camp Peak

are usually available at the TRT kiosk. There is no water or restroom at the trailhead. **Trailhead GPS:** N 38 59.79, W 119 53.73

Miles and Directions

0.0 **START** from the trailhead to the Tahoe Rim Trail. Be prepared for an initial climb and some serious maneuvering over granite rocks.

0.5 Stay on the main trail as it levels out into smooth hard pack with occasional rocky spots—this pretty much defines the rest of this ride. At the rocky step-ups, pick the lines for your return. (**Side trip:** Turn left to the vista point. You needn't feel too compelled; there are vistas all along this ride.)

0.9 Cross an OHV trail and continue on the singletrack. Watch for the blue TRT markers on trees along the way.

5.2 Cross Forest Road 14N33. Up ahead you will skirt Genoa Peak and its radio towers. The rock hopping is behind you. Enjoy a section of smooth trail through the trees. (**Bailout:** Turn right and then right again at the next major intersection to ride FR 14N32 back to the parking lot. Watch out for motorized traffic.)

6.1 You will see the dirt road leading to Genoa Peak on the right. As you approach the ridge of South Camp Peak, the trail makes a final ascent through sections of loose and crumbly rocks.

6.6 Arrive at The Bench on the left side of the trail, with the unobstructed view of Lake Tahoe, Heavenly ski area, Freel Peak, Emerald Bay, the Desolation Wilderness, Granite Chief

Wilderness, and more. The trail is nearly level along the broad ridge; explore a bit before returning the way you came. The actual South Camp Peak is an outcropping of rocks east of the trail. (**Option:** Continue 5.6 miles to Spooner Summit for an extended out-and-back or, if you planned ahead, a shuttle pickup.)

13.2 Arrive back at the trailhead.

17 Kingsbury Grade to Big Meadow Point-to-Point

Bring plenty of water and a camera for a day's trek along the southern section of the Tahoe Rim Trail. While you will encounter hikers at the beginning and end of this ride, the traffic thins in the middle. Spectacular views of Lake Tahoe, Carson Valley, and lofty peaks follow as you move in and out of the timberline. The highest point on the trail is at 9,730 feet and just below Freel Peak—the highest peak in Tahoe. Spur trails to the peak are not accessible to bikes. Picturesque Star Lake sits at the foot of Jobs Sister—second highest peak in Tahoe—and makes an ideal spot for lunch. There are many variations to this ride: An out-and-back to Star Lake is popular. Many riders start from Big Meadow, but most drop down at Saxon Creek or ride an out-and-back to Freel Peak. The trail itself offers plenty of diversity—from hard-packed and smooth trail to staircased granite boulders. There is little slacking on this route; when there is a reprieve in the climb, the coarse sand of the decomposing granite emerges.

Start: From the parking lot to the Stagecoach lift on the Nevada side of Heavenly Mountain Resort
Distance: 22.8-mile point-to-point
Approximate riding time: 5½ to 6 hours
Difficulty rating: Difficult due to distance, strenuous climbs, and rugged terrain; sections of sand and unrideable rocks
Trail surface: Singletrack
Seasons: Mid-July through October
Other trail users: Hikers and equestrians
Land status: Lake Tahoe Basin Management Unit
Nearest town: South Lake Tahoe, California

Fees and permits: No fees or permits required
Schedule: 24 hours a day
Maps: Maptech CD: California, High Sierra/Tahoe; USGS maps: South Lake Tahoe, CA; Freel Peak, CA; Tahoe Rim Trail, Big Meadow–Kingsbury South Segment
Trail contacts: Lake Tahoe Basin Management Unit, USDA Forest Service, 35 College Drive, South Lake Tahoe, CA 96150; (530) 543-2600; www.fs.fed.us/r5/ltbmu. Tahoe Rim Trail Association: Incline Village, NV; (775) 298-0012; www.tahoerimtrail.org.

Finding the trailhead: From South Lake Tahoe and Stateline, take Nevada Highway 207 (Kingsbury Grade) east 3.2 miles to Daggett Summit. Turn right onto Tramway Drive at Summit Village–Heavenly. Veer left at Jack Drive and follow the signs to Stagecoach Lodge. Veer right as the road becomes one-way. Turn left down Quaking Aspen Lane to the parking area. The ride begins next to the Stagecoach Express chairlift and trailhead to the Tahoe Rim Trail. There is no

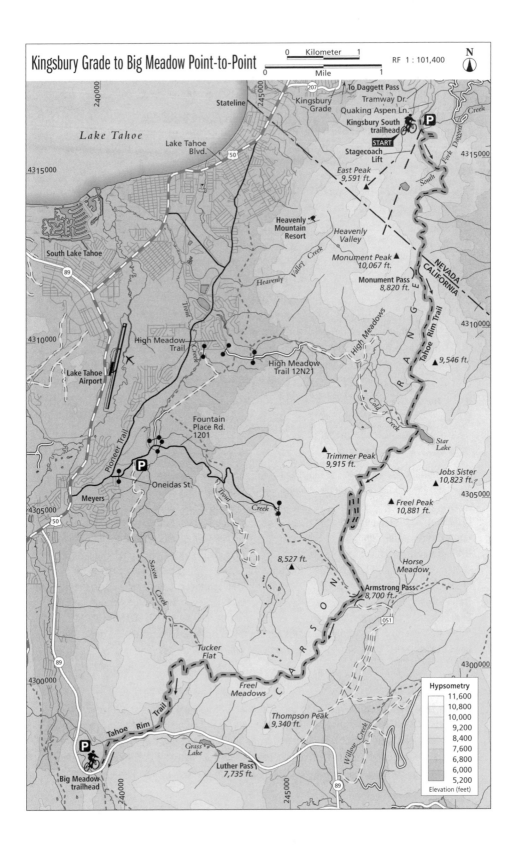

Kingsbury Grade to Big Meadow Point-to-Point

0 — Kilometer — 1
0 — Mile — 1

RF 1 : 101,400

N

Lake Tahoe

Stateline

Kingsbury Grade

To Daggett Pass
Tramway Dr.
Quaking Aspen Ln.
Kingsbury South trailhead
START
Stagecoach Lift

East Peak 9,591 ft.

Lake Tahoe Blvd.

50

240000
245000
4315000

South Lake Tahoe

89

Heavenly Mountain Resort

Heavenly Valley

Heavenly Valley Creek

Monument Peak ▲ 10,067 ft.

Monument Pass 8,820 ft.

NEVADA
CALIFORNIA

South Fork Daggett Creek

Tahoe Rim Trail

4310000

High Meadow Trail

Trout Creek

High Meadow Trail 12N21

High Meadows

▲ 9,546 ft.

Cold Creek

Star Lake

Lake Tahoe Airport

Pioneer Trail

Fountain Place Rd. 1201

Trimmer Peak 9,915 ft.

Jobs Sister ▲ 10,823 ft.

4305000

P

Oneidas St.

Meyers

Trout Creek

8,527 ft. ▲

▲ Freel Peak 10,881 ft.

Saxon Creek

Horse Meadow

C A R S O N

Armstrong Pass 8,700 ft.

051

Tucker Flat

Freel Meadows

4300000

Tahoe Rim Trail

Thompson Peak ▲ 9,340 ft.

Willow Creek

89

P

Big Meadow trailhead

Grass Lake

Luther Pass 7,735 ft.

89

R A N G E

Hypsometry

	11,600
	10,800
	10,000
	9,200
	8,400
	7,600
	6,800
	6,000
	5,200

Elevation (feet)

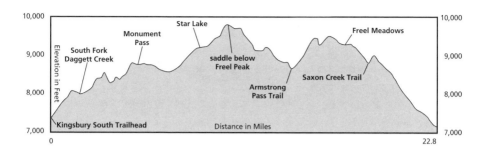

water or restroom at the parking lot. Maps are usually available at the TRT information board. **Trailhead GPS:** N 38 57.63, W 119 53.23

Miles and Directions

0.0 **START** from the trailhead to the Tahoe Rim Trail and climb. The trail is well marked with the blue TRT symbols along the way.

0.3 Cross the dirt road and veer left on the singletrack through the meadow and into the forest.

1.3 Arrive at the top of a saddle. Just beyond, veer left at the fork.

1.8 After a stream crossing, climb through the fir forest and maneuver over granite boulders.

3.3 Reach a dirt road, where you veer right and head steeply downhill.

3.5 As the road bends sharply to the left, turn right onto the singletrack Tahoe Rim Trail and start regaining elevation. Perhaps without noticing, you will pass under one of Heavenly's ski lifts.

4.0 You have climbed out of the trees to a grand view and dramatic drop to Carson Valley. Naturally, the trail gets steeper up ahead with switchbacks.

5.1 Reach Monument Pass and follow the sign to Star Lake. The trail descends a bit and is sandy, as in very slow going when it's dry. The open landscape presents Lake Tahoe and Desolation Wilderness.

8.4 Catch the first view of Star Lake and continue straight to it; do not turn right at the trail leading downhill. (**Bailout:** Turn right and drop down to the High Meadow Trail and eventually Pioneer Trail in South Lake Tahoe.)

8.5 Arrive at Star Lake. Savor. When it's time to press on, head counterclockwise around the end of lake. There is a water crossing at the outlet. As you leave the lake, a sign will lead you straight ahead and through the rocks.

9.5 The trail gets rockier and the trees fewer. As you near the summit, heed the signs to stay on the trail through the sensitive plant area.

10.3 Reach the saddle and highest point on the ride, with Freel Peak looming overhead. Greet downhill switchbacks and creek crossings.

13.3 Arrive at Armstrong Pass. Turn right, following the TRT sign to BIG MEADOW. (**FYI:** Forest Road 051 comes in on left and is an alternate route to California Highway 89.)

13.4 Continue straight on the TRT at the junction to Fountain Place Road. (**Bailout:** Turn right and ride down to Fountain Place Road and Pioneer Trail.)

15.1 The trail levels off along the ridge for sweeping views of Hope Valley to the south.

15.9 Pass all the edge of Freel Meadows.

16.2 Just beyond the summit, arrive at yet another magnificent overlook of Lake Tahoe.

18.2 Reach the junction with Saxon Creek Trail and continue straight to Big Meadow. (**Option:** If you have it in you, turn right down the infamous Mr. Toad's Wild Ride.)

18.7 Reach a saddle and end of the last climb.

20.7 Continue straight to Big Meadow at the fork to Grass Lake on the left. Enjoy the clean sweep downhill.

22.2 Balance across the creek on the log.

22.7 Turn left at the pavement. Up ahead, turn right at the gate into the Big Meadow parking lot.

22.8 Arrive at the TRT information board and restrooms.

18 Power Line Loop

Get out of town quickly with this ride along the edge of South Lake Tahoe. Smooth singletrack follows the contours at the base of the mountains rising above Heavenly Valley. There are no long climbs, just undulating trail with several short rises; the biggest challenge is moving into the correct chain ring. Ride this as a loop, returning along the paved Pioneer Trail thoroughfare, or as an out-and-back entirely on singletrack. A portion of the ride is accessible to motorcycles and ATVs and gets dusty and chewed up by summer. This is balanced by a quiet meander along Trout Creek near the turnaround point. Most of the ride is through the shaded pine forest, with clearings along the way that offer views of Freel Peak and Lake Tahoe. Expect some seasonal creek crossings. This is an easy connect for other rides up Cold Creek and Fountain Place Road.

Start: Near the top of Ski Run Boulevard, South Lake Tahoe

Distance: 15.0-mile loop or 14.8-mile out-and-back

Approximate riding time: 1½ to 2 hours

Difficulty rating: Moderate—due to distance and varied terrain

Trail surface: 51 percent paved road, 38 percent singletrack, and 11 percent dirt road

Seasons: May through October

Other trail users: Hikers, joggers, and vehicles

Land status: Lake Tahoe Basin Management Unit

Nearest town: South Lake Tahoe, California

Fees and permits: No fees or permits required

Schedule: 24 hours a day

Maps: Maptech CD: California, High Sierra/Tahoe; USGS maps: South Lake Tahoe, CA; Freel Peak, CA

Trail contact: Lake Tahoe Basin Management Unit, USDA Forest Service, 35 College Drive, South Lake Tahoe, CA 96150; (530) 543-2600; www.fs.fed.us/r5/ltbmu

Starting out on Power Line Trail ▶

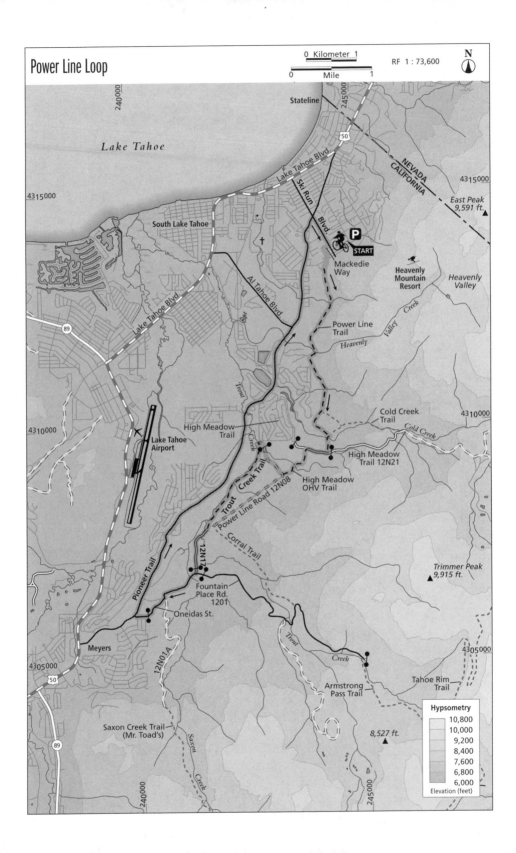

Power Line Loop

0　Kilometer　1

0　Mile　1

RF 1 : 73,600

N

Stateline

Lake Tahoe

240000

245000

4315000

East Peak
9,591 ft. ▲

NEVADA
CALIFORNIA

50

Lake Tahoe Blvd.

South Lake Tahoe

4315000

Ski Run Blvd.

P

START

Mackedie
Way

Heavenly
Mountain
Resort

Heavenly
Valley

Al Tahoe Blvd.

Lake Tahoe Blvd.

89

Valley Creek

Power Line
Trail

Heavenly

Trout

High Meadow
Trail

Creek

Cold Creek
Trail

4310000

Cold Creek

Lake Tahoe
Airport

4310000

High Meadow
Trail 12N21

Trout Creek Trail

High Meadow
OHV Trail

Power Line Road 12N08

Corral Trail

12N17

Trimmer Peak
9,915 ft. ▲

Pioneer Trail

Fountain
Place Rd.
1201

Oneidas St.

4305000

Meyers

12N01A

50

Trout

Creek

4305000

Tahoe Rim
Trail

Armstrong
Pass Trail

89

Saxon Creek Trail
(Mr. Toad's)

Saxon Creek

8,527 ft. ▲

Hypsometry

10,800
10,000
9,200
8,400
7,600
6,800
6,000
Elevation (feet)

Snowcapped mountains through the trees

Finding the trailhead: From South Lake Tahoe, drive up Ski Run Boulevard toward Heavenly Mountain Resort and turn right onto Saddle Road. Although the ride begins at the end of Saddle Road, there is no parking near the trailhead. Park on Mackedie Way, the last street on the right before the trailhead. There is no water or restroom at the trailhead. **Trailhead GPS:** N 38 55.99, W 119 56.97

Miles and Directions

0.0 **START** from the unsigned Power Line trailhead at the end of Saddle Road. Immediately veer left at the first fork, under the power lines. Almost immediately you will come to a wide dirt road; jog to the left as you cross the road and continue on the singletrack on the other side. It's easy to miss the wooden POWER LINE sign. This may sound confusing—welcome to Power Line Trail! There are many side trails on this ride, but the main route is usually obvious. Ignore the vague spur trails and fading jeep roads. It will all be clearer on the next trip.

1.3 Continue straight, following the sign to POWER LINE TRAIL, TR18E33. (**Bailout:** Turn right at the unsigned fork to Al Tahoe Boulevard.)

1.8 Follow the trail signs, riding under the power lines. Unless you're ready to bail on the ride, ignore a series of trails on the right to the nearby neighborhood.

2.4 Continue straight at the junction with Cold Creek Trail to High Meadow on the left.

3.1 Turn right, cross the bridge over Cold Creek, and veer left on the other side.

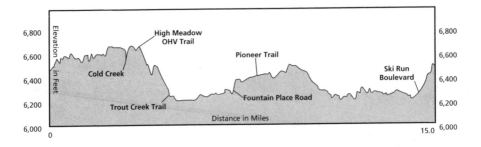

3.4 Ride through the small parking area and High Meadow trailhead. Turn right onto the unsigned dirt High Meadow Road, Forest Road 12N21. (**Option:** Turn left for a loop of Cold Creek.)

3.7 Turn left on the High Meadow OHV Trail and Power Line Road 12N081. The banked turns on this trail are great when not shredded to dust by the traffic. (**Bailout:** Continue straight to Pioneer Trail.)

4.5 Turn right onto the Power Line Road, now Forest Road 12N08.

5.2 The road ends at the paved cul-de-sac on Columbine Trail. Turn left onto the unsigned trail through the split-rail fence. This is a pleasant meander along Trout Creek through meadows and a regenerating pine forest.

6.7 Just past the fence, merge right back on Power Line Road and cross Trout Creek.

6.9 Turn left at the fork onto Forest Road 12N17.

7.4 Turn right at the gate onto the paved Fountain Place Road. This will turn into Oneidas Street. (**Option:** This is the turnaround point for the out-and-back.)

8.3 Turn right onto Pioneer Trail, and watch for traffic.

14.3 Turn right up Ski Run Boulevard.

14.7 Turn right onto Mackedie Way and then right onto Saddle Road to complete the loop.

15.0 Arrive back at the trailhead.

19 Cold Creek Loop

The lower Cold Creek Trail is a popular and easily accessible ride out of South Lake Tahoe. It begins with a ride up the graded High Meadow Road. After less than 2 miles, the loop segment crosses Cold Creek and heads downstream on smooth, well-packed singletrack. Real hammerheads can continue up the painfully steep climb to Star Lake. This ride makes a nice side trip off the Power Line Trail.

Start: From the end of High Meadow Trail off Pioneer Trail

Distance: 3.8-mile loop

Approximate riding time: 45 minutes

Difficulty rating: Moderate—gradual climb and smooth singletrack

Trail surface: 60 percent dirt road and 40 percent singletrack

Seasons: July (when streams are fordable) though October

Other trail users: Hikers, equestrians, and dogs

Land status: Lake Tahoe Basin Management Unit

Nearest town: South Lake Tahoe, California

Fees and permits: No fees or permits required

Schedule: 24 hours a day

Maps: Maptech CD: California, High Sierra/ Tahoe; USGS map: South Lake Tahoe, CA

Trail contacts: Lake Tahoe Basin Management Unit, USDA Forest Service, 35 College Drive, South Lake Tahoe, CA 96150; (530) 543-2600; www.fs.fed.us/r5/ltbmu

Finding the trailhead: From South Lake Tahoe, take High Meadow Trail off Pioneer Trail. (This is 2.5 miles south of Ski Run Boulevard and just before the school on the left.) Drive to the end of the pavement on High Meadow Trail and park; this is where the directions begin. Alternatively, if the gate is open you can drive to the High Meadow trailhead. There is no restroom or water at the trailhead. **Trailhead GPS:** N 38 53.88, W 119 57.45

Miles and Directions

0.0 **START** from the gate at the end of the paved High Meadow Trail. Follow gravel Forest Road 12N21; this will take you up to the turnaround point.

0.3 Pass the High Meadow OHV Trail on the right.

0.6 Arrive at the official High Meadow trailhead and continue up the road. You will return to this spot to complete the loop.

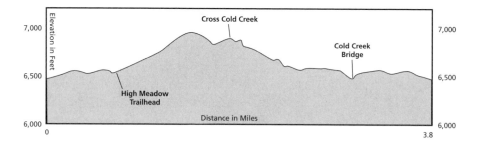

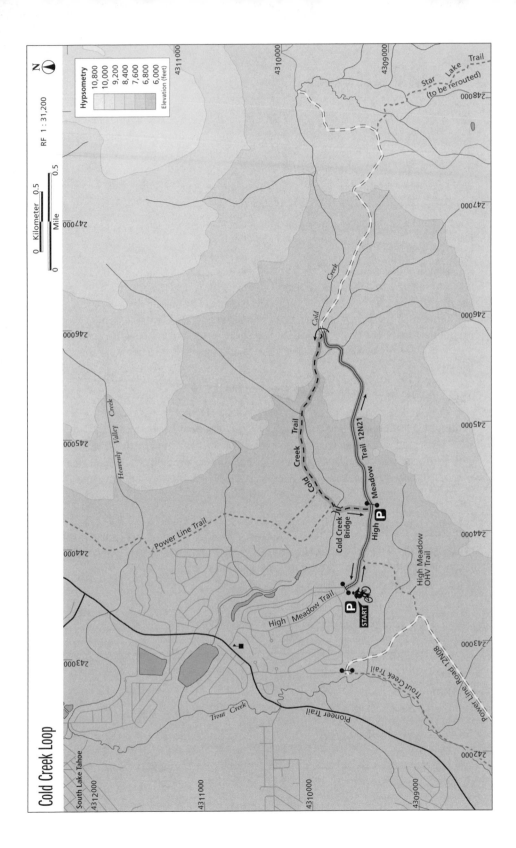

Cold Creek Loop

RF 1 : 31,200

Hypsometry
- 10,800
- 10,000
- 9,200
- 8,400
- 7,600
- 6,800
- 6,000

Elevation (feet)

Star Lake Trail (to be rerouted)

Cold Creek

Cold Creek Trail

Power Line Trail

Heavenly Valley Creek

High Meadow Trail 12N21

Cold Creek Bridge

High Meadow

High Meadow OHV Trail

High Meadow Trail

START

Trout Creek Trail

Power Line Road 12N08

Pioneer Trail

Trout Creek

South Lake Tahoe

Cool bridge over Cold Creek

1.3 Reach the top of the first hill. You will cross a couple of streams before the turnoff.

1.7 Turn left on the singletrack and cross Cold Creek. If the creek is not fordable, look for a loose makeshift log bridge through the trees on the right. Once across the creek, turn left and head downstream.

2.5 Veer left at the fork. The trail on the right is a connector to Power Line Trail.

2.9 Turn left, joining Power Line Trail; cross the bridge, and veer left again on the other side.

3.2 Pull into the High Meadow trailhead, completing the loop. Turn right and return down the dirt road.

3.8 Arrive back at the start.

20 Corral Trail Loop

One of several easily accessible rides off Pioneer Trail in South Lake Tahoe. Ride the paved Fountain Place Road up to the Corral Trail for a quick singletrack fix. Enjoy smooth, meandering turns and whoop-de-dos through open forest. For the most part, the trail is smooth and well packed, with some sandy and rocky patches. All-terrain vehicles share this popular path; watch for them. This is one of the first trails to open in spring, and it gets pounded to a fine dust by the end of summer. The bottom of Corral Trail connects with Power Line Trail to extend your trip. Word has it that the Corral Trail will be extended; stay tuned!

Start: From Fountain Place Road off Pioneer Trail

Distance: 5.9-mile loop

Approximate riding time: 1 hour

Difficulty rating: Moderate—for the climb

Trail surface: 52 percent paved road, 34 percent singletrack, and 14 percent dirt road

Seasons: May through October

Other trail users: Hikers and off-highway vehicles

Land status: Lake Tahoe Basin Management Unit

Nearest town: Meyers, California

Fees and permits: No fees or permits required

Schedule: 24 hours a day

Maps: Maptech CD: California, High Sierra/Tahoe; USGS maps: South Lake Tahoe, CA; Freel Peak, CA

Trail contact: Lake Tahoe Basin Management Unit, USDA Forest Service, 35 College Drive, South Lake Tahoe, CA 96150; (530) 543-2600, www.fs.fed.us/r5/ltbmu

Finding the trailhead: From Meyers, take U.S. Highway 50 north and turn right onto Pioneer Trail toward South Lake Tahoe. After 0.8 mile, turn right onto Oneidas Street. This short street ends at the gate to Forest Road 1201. If the gate is closed, start here. Otherwise follow the paved Fountain Place Road, signed SINGLE LANE ROUGH ROAD, to a small parking area about 0.5 mile down on the right. There is an information board but no details for this ride. Don't expect water or a restroom. **Trailhead GPS:** N 38 52.10, W 119 59.39

Miles and Directions

0.0 **START** from the small parking lot and continue up the Fountain Place Road. Ignore all side gates and trails; you will climb on the pavement for 2.6 miles.

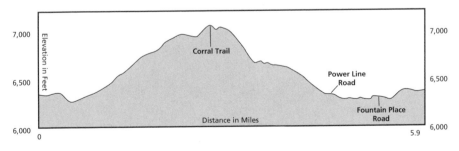

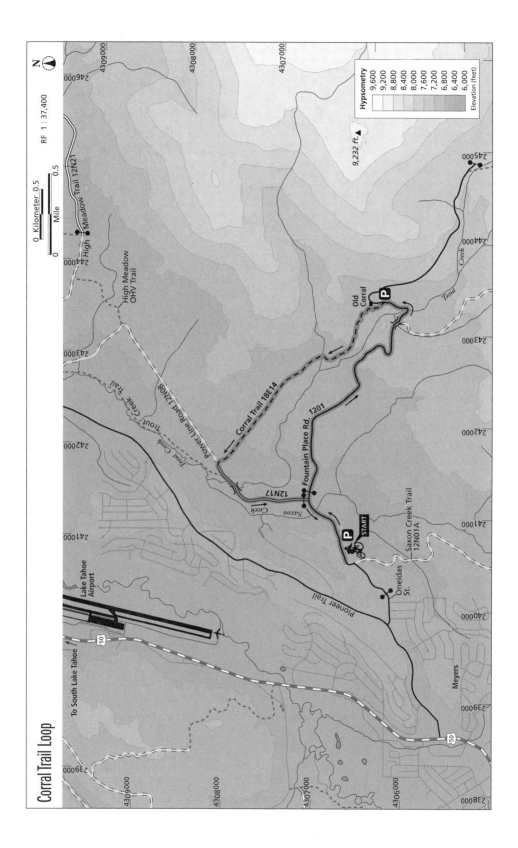

Corral Trail Loop

Head 'em up, roll 'em out on Corral Trail

0.5 Continue up the pavement, bypassing Forest Road 12N17 on the left. You will complete the loop there on the return. In 100 yards, pass another gate.

2.2 Just past the bridge, veer left at the fork in the road.

2.6 Reach the trailhead to Corral Trail—OHV (off-highway vehicle) Trail 18E14. Remains of an old corral are next to the trailhead. Turn left and enjoy.

4.6 Turn left onto Power Line Road, Forest Road 12N08.

4.9 Turn left past the paved bridge over Trout Creek onto FR 12N17. This is signed as the designated route for OHVs.

5.4 Turn right at Fountain Place Road, completing the loop.

5.9 Arrive back at the start.

21 Armstrong Pass to Saxon Creek Loop

Saxon Creek Trail is more commonly known as Mr. Toad's Wild Ride. Noted for its wild downhill, this is one of the legendary trails in Tahoe. There are several ways to access Mr. Toad's, but this loop eliminates a shuttle and minimizes the road riding. The first 3.0 miles up the paved Fountain Place Road are on a route that was one man's dream for the main pass over the mountains. Today the ride from the end of the road to the ridge follows some beautiful and well-graded singletrack that connects to the Tahoe Rim Trail (TRT) at Armstrong Pass. An out-and-back to Armstrong Pass is a great ride in itself.

It's a bit of a huff along the TRT to Saxon Creek Trail, but the views along the rim are gorgeous. The descent on Mr. Toad's is extreme: steep, technical, nicely banked turns, concrete lattice trail work, and some impossible drops. Mr. Toad's is for advanced riders with the good sense to walk the crazy stuff.

Start: From Fountain Place Road off Pioneer Trail

Distance: 17.7-mile loop

Approximate riding time: 4 to 4½ hours

Difficulty rating: Difficult—long climb and steep descent; extreme rocks, drops, boulders, and long staircase

Trail surface: 68 percent singletrack, 22 percent paved road, and 10 percent dirt road

Seasons: Late June through October

Other trail users: Hikers, equestrians, and OHVs

Land status: Lake Tahoe Basin Management Unit

Nearest town: Meyers, California

Fees and permits: No fees or permits required

Schedule: 24 hours a day

Maps: Maptech CD: California, High Sierra/Tahoe; USGS map: Freel Peak, CA; Tahoe Rim Trail, Big Meadow to Kingsbury South Segment

Trail contacts: Lake Tahoe Basin Management Unit, USDA Forest Service, 35 College Drive, South Lake Tahoe, CA 96150; (530) 543-2600; www.fs.fed.us/r5/ltbmu. Tahoe Rim Trail Association, Incline Village, NV 89451; (775) 298-0012; www.tahoerimtrail.org.

Finding the trailhead: From Meyers, take U.S. Highway 50 north and turn right onto Pioneer Trail toward South Lake Tahoe. After 0.8 mile, turn right onto Oneidas Street. This short street ends at the gate to Forest Road 1201. If the gate is closed, start here. Otherwise follow the paved Fountain Place Road, signed SINGLE LANE ROUGH ROAD, to a small parking area about 0.5 mile down on the right. The loop ends on the dirt road from the parking area—Forest Road 12N01A. There is an information board, but don't expect any details for this ride. There is no water or restroom at the trailhead. **Trailhead GPS:** N 38 52.10, W 119 59.39

Miles and Directions

0.0 START from the small parking lot, and continue up the paved Fountain Place Road. Ignore all side gates and trails; you will climb the road for nearly 4.0 miles.

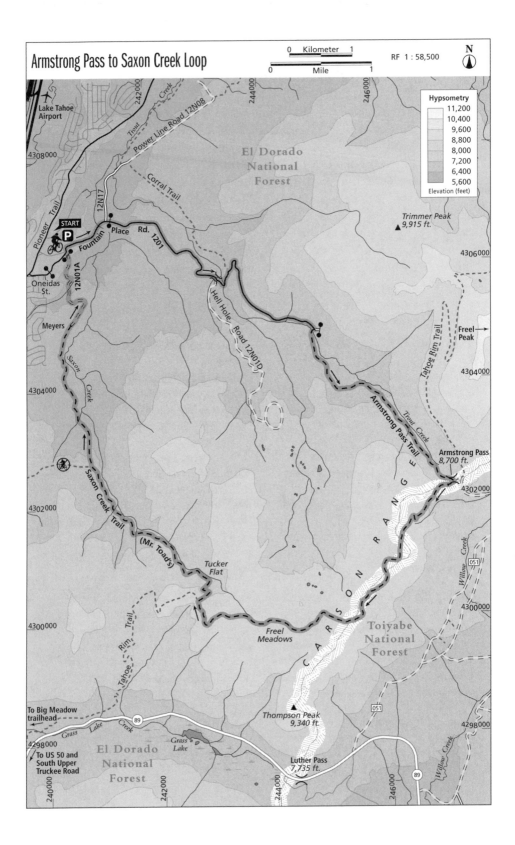

Armstrong Pass to Saxon Creek Loop

RF 1 : 58,500

N

Hypsometry
11,200
10,400
9,600
8,800
8,000
7,200
6,400
5,600
Elevation (feet)

Lake Tahoe Airport

Power Line Road 12N08

El Dorado National Forest

Trout Creek

Corral Trail

Pioneer Trail

12N17

START
P

Place Rd. 1201
Fountain

Oneidas St.

12N01A

Meyers

Saxon Creek

Hell Hole Road 12N01D

Trimmer Peak
9,915 ft.

Tahoe Rim Trail

Freel Peak

Armstrong Pass Trail

Trout Creek

Armstrong Pass
8,700 ft.

Saxon Creek Trail

(Mr. Toad's)

Tucker Flat

CARSON RANGE

Willow Creek

051

Tahoe Rim Trail

Freel Meadows

Toiyabe National Forest

To Big Meadow trailhead

Grass Lake Creek

89

Grass Lake

Thompson Peak
9,340 ft.

051

To US 50 and South Upper Truckee Road

El Dorado National Forest

Luther Pass
7,735 ft.

89

Willow Creek

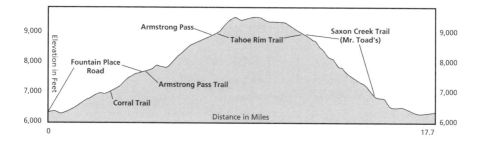

0.5 Ride past the gate, and continue on the paved road.

2.2 Just past the bridge, veer left at the fork. (**Side trip:** The right fork is Hell Hole Road, Forest Road 12N01D.)

2.6 The climb gets steeper just beyond the trailhead to Corral Trail on the left, OHV Trail 18E14. (**Bailout:** If you are having second thoughts, turn left and follow this sweet single-track. At the bottom, turn left onto Power Line Road and left again onto Forest Road 12N17 back to Fountain Place Road.)

3.9 The road ends with the pavement and gated private property. Turn right onto the single-track Armstrong Pass Trail. There's an immediate fork; veer right. If you miss it, don't worry, the paths rejoin up ahead. This beautiful, sweeping trail is a welcome change from the paved road.

6.8 Arrive at Armstrong Pass and turn right onto the Tahoe Rim Trail. Mentally prepare for more climbing. (**Option:** Turn around and enjoy the cruise home.)

8.5 The trail levels off along the ridge for full views of Hope Valley to the south.

9.5 Just beyond the summit, arrive at an overlook and the ride's best view of Lake Tahoe.

11.6 Lower the seat, and turn right at the signed Saxon Creek Trail—aka Mr. Toad's. After the first 0.5 mile, the trail gets extreme.

14.0 For the fine art of trail building, check out the granite-slab bridge and stairway.

14.5 Reach the end of the pristine section. By the end of the season, this lower trail gets dusty.

16.0 Veer right at the fork. The trail flattens out and eventually becomes a dirt road.

17.4 Continue straight through the monster gravel, ignoring the road merging from the left. In fact, ignore all side roads and steady your course straight on the main road, FR 12N01A.

17.7 Arrive back at the parking lot. Go home and read Kenneth Grahame's *The Wind in the Willows*.

Alternate access to Mr. Toad's: Start in Meyers and ride the South Upper Truckee Road (5.7 miles) or California Highway 89 (5.5 miles of high-speed traffic) to the Tahoe Rim Trail's Big Meadow trailhead. This is also the drop-off point for a shuttle ride. Ride the TRT northeast 4.6 miles to the top of Saxon Creek Trail.

22 Big Meadow to Pacific Crest Trail Out-and-Back

This is one of the best rides on the Tahoe Rim Trail (TRT). Despite a ragged start, the generally smooth and hard-packed trail passes through pine forests, stands of aspen, and meadows with intermittent patches of rocks. In June and July the wild-flowers are magnificent in Big Meadow and Meiss Meadows. Dramatic volcanic boulders tower over the trail as it runs along Round Lake. The turnaround point is in a beautiful valley at the junction with the Pacific Crest Trail. Here an old cowboy cabin adds to the high-country feeling. The side trip to Dardanelles Lake is more technical but worth the effort. Expert riders can turn this into a loop with the steep and loose downhill run on Christmas Valley Trail. Mind your manners; the lakes are popular destinations for hikers.

Start: From Big Meadow Trailhead on California Highway 89

Distance: 10.8-mile out-and-back

Approximate riding time: 2 to 2½ hours

Difficulty rating: Moderate climb with some technical and rocky sections to maneuver

Trail surface: Singletrack

Seasons: Late June to October

Other trail users: Hikers and equestrians

Land status: Lake Tahoe Basin Management Unit

Nearest town: South Lake Tahoe, California

Fees and permits: No fees or permits required

Schedule: 24 hours a day

Maps: Maptech CD: California, High Sierra/Tahoe; USGS maps: Freel Peak, CA; Caples Lake, CA; Tahoe Rim Trail, Big Meadow–Echo Lake Segment

Trail contacts: Lake Tahoe Basin Management Unit, USDA Forest Service, 35 College Drive, South Lake Tahoe, CA 96150; (530) 543-2600; www.fs.fed.us/r5/ltbmu. Tahoe Rim Trail Association: Incline Village, NV 89451; (775) 298-0012; www.tahoerimtrail.org.

Finding the trailhead: From South Lake Tahoe, drive south on U.S. Highway 50 to Meyers and turn left (south) onto CA 89 toward Luther Pass. Turn left into the Big Meadow trailhead parking lot, about 5.2 miles from US 50. Maps are usually available at the TRT kiosk. There are restrooms but no water. **Trailhead GPS:** N 38 47.32, W 120 00.04

Miles and Directions

0.0 **START** from the lower end of the parking lot at the trailhead to the Tahoe Rim Trail south to Round Valley. A short trail takes you over to CA 89.

0.1 Cross the highway and head up the well-marked singletrack. The trail is particularly rocky and steep for the next 0.4 mile. There is no shame in carrying your bike.

0.6 Just beyond the gate, the trail forks. Veer right for the ride through Big Meadow. The climbing resumes at the end of the meadow. (**Option:** Turn left and check out Scott's Lake. Less striking than the other lakes, there is also less traffic here. A dirt road from the lake leads down to Hope Valley.)

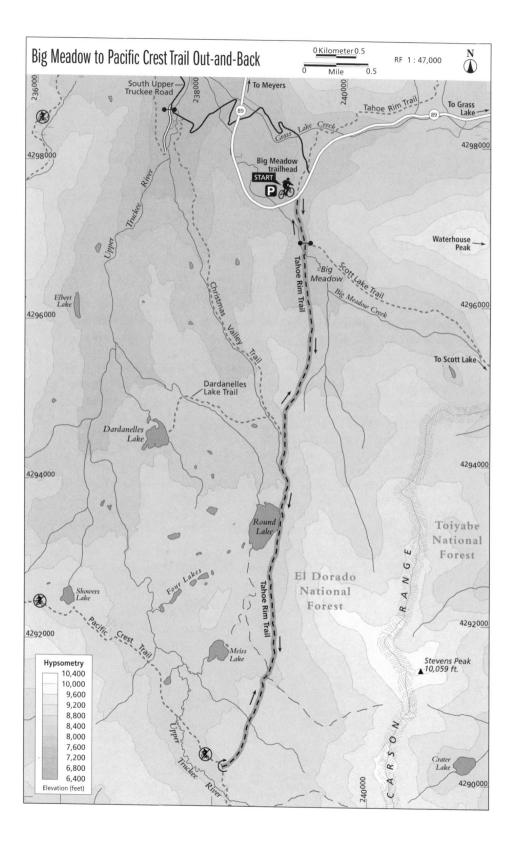

Big Meadow to Pacific Crest Trail Out-and-Back

Kilometer 0.5
0 **Mile** 0.5
RF 1 : 47,000

N

South Upper Truckee Road
To Meyers
Tahoe Rim Trail
To Grass Lake
89
89

Grass Lake Creek

236000
238000
240000

4298000

Big Meadow trailhead
START
P

Waterhouse Peak

Tahoe Rim Trail
Big Meadow
Scott Lake Trail
Big Meadow Creek

Upper Truckee River

Elbert Lake

Christmas Valley Trail

4296000

To Scott Lake

Dardanelles Lake Trail

Dardanelles Lake

4294000

Round Lake

Toiyabe National Forest

Four Lakes

Showers Lake

Tahoe Rim Trail

El Dorado National Forest

C A R S O N   R A N G E

Pacific Crest Trail

4292000

Meiss Lake

Stevens Peak
▲ 10,059 ft.

Hypsometry

	10,400
	10,000
	9,600
	9,200
	8,800
	8,400
	8,000
	7,600
	7,200
	6,800
	6,400

Elevation (feet)

Upper Truckee River

Crater Lake

240000

4290000

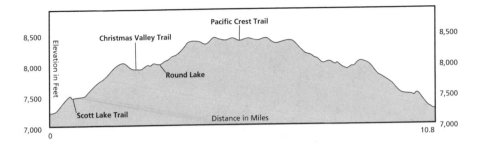

2.1 Arrive at a minor summit for a downhill reprieve.

2.4 Veer left at the junction to Round Lake. (**Side trip:** Now or later, turn right and follow the signs to Dardanelles Lake. Expect some hike-a-bike sections and seasonal stream crossings en route to this gorgeous lake; it's worth the 2.8-mile detour. Giant granite slabs are perched along the edge of the lake and provide a popular picnic spot.)

3.1 You've reached Round Lake. Continue left along the east side of the lake and on toward Meiss Meadows. (**Side trip:** Try the narrow singletrack to the right around the lake for a quick swim and a better view of volcanic outcroppings towering above the lake.)

5.4 Reach the T intersection with the Pacific Crest Trail and the end of the road for bikes. Enjoy the picturesque alpine valley, meadow, and headwaters of the Upper Truckee River before turning around and retracing your tracks. If you were on foot, you could turn left to Mexico or right to Canada. Too bad.

7.8 Return to Round Lake.

8.4 Arrive back at the junction with Christmas Valley Trail. Veer right to stay on the TRT and return to Big Meadow. (**Side trip:** Last chance to visit Dardanelles Lake. **Loop option:** Expert riders can take the Christmas Valley Trail for a 2.5-mile, steep, rocky, and loose drop 1,400 feet down to the Upper Truckee River. This is not a trail to be ridden uphill. At the bottom of the singletrack, turn right onto the dirt road. In 0.2 mile, turn right onto the paved South Upper Truckee Road. Climb 2.0 miles up the old highway to the Big Meadow parking lot. Halfway up you will cross CA 89. Don't expect any signs along the way.)

10.8 Arrive back at Big Meadow parking lot.

23 Burnside Lake Out-and-Back

Burnside Lake is a pleasant place to swim, fish, canoe, and, as evidenced by the camping around the lake, generally hang. The ride is on a wide and generally smooth dirt road, with sections of serious washboard from the traffic. This is a good place to build endurance without any technical challenges and enjoy the view of the Carson Range along the way. Be warned; the intermittent traffic means eating some dust. For peak baggers, there is a hill-climb to Hawkins Peak along the way. From the lake, there's a rugged trail you can hike or ride to an overlook of Grover Hot Springs and Markleeville 2,600 feet below. The ride earns its mark for the picturesque lake and fun downhill ride home. If you want to give the kids a mountain biking thrill, drive them to the lake and let them ride back.

Start: From the junction of California Highways 89 and 88

Distance: 11.0-mile out-and-back

Approximate riding time: 2 to 3 hours

Difficulty rating: Moderate—gradual, steady climb; nontechnical

Trail surface: Dirt road

Seasons: May through October

Other trail users: Vehicles

Land status: Humboldt-Toiyabe National Forest

Nearest town: Meyers, California

Fees and permits: No fees or permits required

Schedule: 24 hours a day

Maps: Maptech CD: California, High Sierra/Tahoe; USGS maps: Freel Peak, CA; Carson, CA

Trail contacts: Humboldt-Toiyabe National Forest, Carson Ranger District, 1536 South Carson Street, Carson City, NV 89701; (775) 882-2766; www.fs.fed.us/r4/htnf

Finding the trailhead: From South Lake Tahoe, drive south on U.S. Highway 50 to Meyers, and turn left (south) onto CA 89 over Luther Pass into Hope Valley. At the junction with CA 88, drive straight into the parking lot for the Hope Valley Wildlife Area. **Trailhead GPS:** N 38 46.54, W 119 55.13

Miles and Directions

0.0 START from the information board at the parking lot. Drive through the gate and follow the Burnside Lake Road, Forest Road 019, to the lake. Ignore all side roads and private

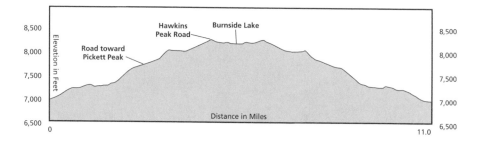

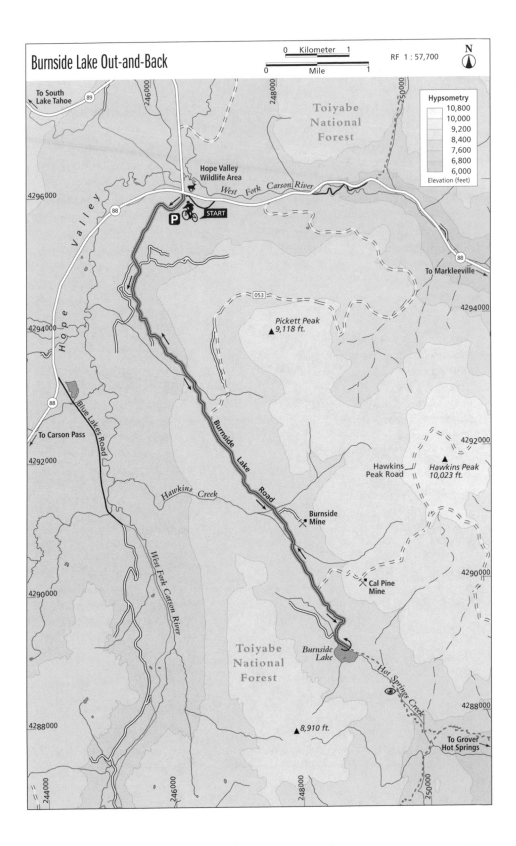

Burnside Lake Out-and-Back

0 Kilometer 1
0 Mile 1

RF 1 : 57,700

N

Hypsometry
10,800
10,000
9,200
8,400
7,600
6,800
6,000
Elevation (feet)

To South Lake Tahoe

89

Toiyabe National Forest

Hope Valley Wildlife Area

West Fork Carson River

4296000

88

P

START

To Markleeville

88

053

4294000

Pickett Peak 9,118 ft.

4294000

Hope Valley

88

To Carson Pass

4292000

Blue Lakes Road

Burnside Lake Road

Hawkins Creek

4292000

Hawkins Peak Road

Hawkins Peak 10,023 ft.

Burnside Mine

West Fork Carson River

4290000

Cal Pine Mine

4290000

Toiyabe National Forest

Burnside Lake

Hot Springs Creek

4288000

8,910 ft.

To Grover Hot Springs

4288000

244000

246000

248000

250000

roads along the way. Unfortunately, you can't rely on the few signs there are. If you come to Forest Road 610, stand on your head to read it correctly.

0.4 Bypass the uphill road on the left.

0.9 Continue straight across the cattleguard at the junction with Forest Road 019E on the right; beware of missing letters on signs.

2.7 Ignore Forest Road 053 on the left; this road skirts Pickett Peak.

3.5 Ignore Forest Road 019H on the right.

3.8 Continue straight where a road comes in from the left.

4.7 Bypass the road on the left. (**Option:** Turn left to reach Hawkins Peak. There is no shade up there, so pick your day wisely.)

5.2 Veer left at the junction to reach the lake.

5.5 Arrive at the canoe launch. When it's time, retrace your tracks home. (**Option:** Continue by foot or bike on the road as it becomes a ragged trail. Follow this to an overlook of Charity Valley and the Mokelumne Wilderness beyond.)

11.0 Arrive back at the parking lot.

24 Hawley Grade Point-to-Point

The Hawley Grade National Recreation Trail was once a Pony Express route over Echo Summit. Starting at the top of the grade, it is a dramatic drop to the Upper Truckee River 1,000 feet below. The challenging trail clings to the edge of a slide-prone hillside, with boulders and loose rocks along the way. Striking views of the lake and canyon filter through the forest along the way. Stop now and then to catch the view; you can't take it in while riding this one. The lower section is lush year-round and passes along a small waterfall in early spring. Behave and watch for hikers. Stalwart souls start at the bottom and ride this as an out-and-back. Many do it as a loop.

Start: From U.S. Highway 50 at the top of Meyers Grade

Distance: 2.1-mile point-to-point

Approximate riding time: 15 to 30 minutes

Difficulty rating: Difficult—steep grade, loose rocks, wicked steps; all on the edge

Trail surface: Singletrack

Seasons: Late June through October

Other trail users: Hikers

Land status: Lake Tahoe Basin Management Unit

Nearest town: Meyers, California

Fees and permits: No fees or permits required

Schedule: 24 hours a day

Maps: Maptech CD: California, High Sierra/Tahoe; USGS map: Echo Lake, CA

Trail contacts: Lake Tahoe Basin Management Unit, USDA Forest Service, 35 College Drive, South Lake Tahoe, CA 96150; (530) 543-2600; www.fs.fed.us/r5/ltbmu

Finding the trailhead: From South Lake Tahoe, drive south on U.S. Highway 50 through Meyers and up to the top of the grade at Echo Summit. Pull into the maintenance station on the

Stepping down Hawley Grade

right to carefully turn around and start back on US 50. The trailhead is on the right before the steep descent back to Lake Tahoe. Turn right onto the unsigned and unpaved Echo Summit Road South just before the CURVE 35 MPH sign. A small trail marker is on the left 30 yards from the highway. **Trailhead GPS:** N 38 48.77, W 120 01.76

Miles and Directions

- **0.0** **START** from the top of Hawley Grade National Recreation Trail. The trail begins with a series of extremely steep rock steps. No, the Pony Express horses didn't race down this part. The historic trail converges from the left just below the rocky staircase.
- **1.8** That's it. The trail widens in front of some cabins.
- **2.0** A Pony Express Station historical marker is on the left.
- **2.1** Arrive at the gate and trailhead on the South Upper Truckee Road.

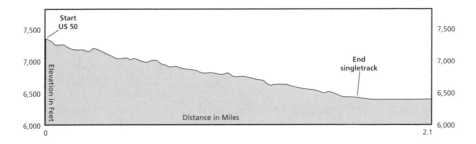

Hawley Grade Point-to-Point

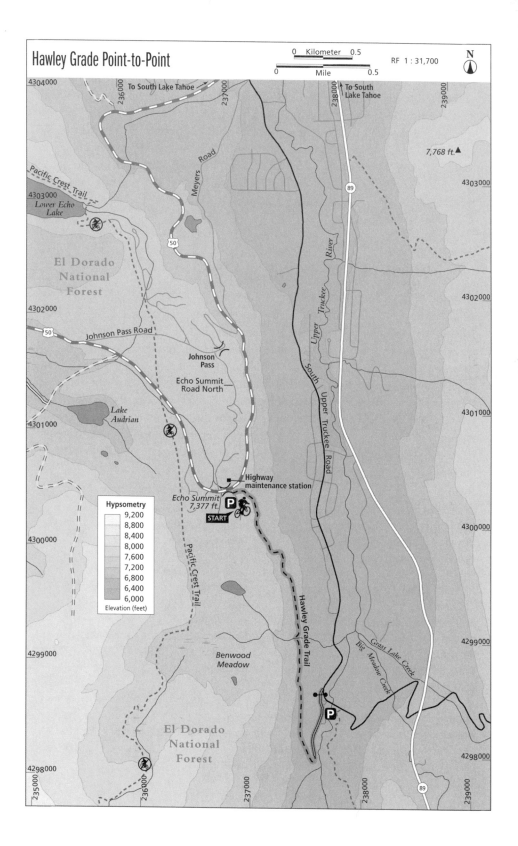

0   Kilometer   0.5

0   Mile   0.5

RF 1 : 31,700

N

4304000

236000

To South Lake Tahoe

237000

238000

To South Lake Tahoe

7,768 ft.▲

239000

Mevers Road

89

4303000

Pacific Crest Trail

Lower Echo Lake

Truckee River

4303000

50

El Dorado National Forest

Upper Truckee River

4302000

4302000

50

Johnson Pass Road

Johnson Pass

South Upper Truckee Road

Echo Summit Road North

Lake Audrian

4301000

4301000

Hypsometry

Elevation (feet)
9,200
8,800
8,400
8,000
7,600
7,200
6,800
6,400
6,000

Highway maintenance station

Echo Summit 7,377 ft.

P

START

4300000

4300000

Pacific Crest Trail

Hawley Grade Trail

4299000

4299000

Benwood Meadow

Grass Lake Creek

Big Meadow Creek

P

4298000

El Dorado National Forest

235000

236000

237000

238000

89

239000

4298000

Loop option: Start on the South Upper Truckee Road at US 50 (this is the last left turn before the climb to the summit). Turn right onto the first road, although unsigned this is Meyers Road/Johnson Grade. Partway up the hill, cross US 50 and continue on the Johnson Pass Road. At the top of the ridge, turn left at the first road and make your way along the unsigned Echo Summit Road North; the biggest challenge is deciding what's driveway and what's road. You will come out at the highway maintenance station on US 50. Turn left and make a right at the first dirt road. The trailhead is on the left. At the bottom of Hawley Grade Trail, turn left onto South Upper Truckee Road and ride back to the start. Loop stats: 10.0 miles in 1 to 2 hours.

25 Washoe Meadows Out-and-Back

Washoe Meadows State Park sits quietly west of the Upper Truckee River from the Lake Tahoe Golf Course. There are no main entrance or trail signs, but lots of flat trails, wildflowers, and big meadow views of Echo Peak and the ridgeline of Desolation Wilderness. This is an easy cruise, with plenty of places to picnic and fish along the first mile. Expect a few annoying sections of sand along the way. The ride runs the length of the meadow and meanders through the woodlands at the northern end. The meadow is being rehabilitated and the forest cleaned up, so routes may change. The northern end of the meadow is swampy in the spring and vulnerable to fat-tire damage. Until things dry out, enjoy the lower meadow and the brilliant view of the snowcapped peaks.

Start: From the end of Chilicothe Street, off North Upper Truckee Road near Meyers

Distance: 5.2-mile out-and-back

Approximate riding time: 45 minutes to an hour

Difficulty rating: Easy—mostly smooth and flat terrain

Trail surface: 50 percent singletrack and 50 percent dirt road

Seasons: July through October

Other trail users: Hikers and equestrians; no dogs allowed

Land status: Washoe Meadows State Park

Nearest town: Meyers, California

Fees and permits: No fees or permits required

Schedule: Daylight hours only

Maps: Maptech CD: California, High Sierra/Tahoe; USGS maps: Echo Lake, CA; Emerald Bay, CA

Trail contact: California State Parks, P.O. Box 266, Tahoma, CA 96142; (530) 525-7232; www.parks.ca.gov

Finding the trailhead: From South Lake Tahoe, head south on U.S. Highway 50 past the inspection station in Meyers. Turn right onto North Upper Truckee Road. Turn right at West San Bernardino Avenue, left on Cholula Street, and left again on Chilicothe Street. The ride begins at the end of the street. **Trailhead GPS:** N 38 51.56, W120 01.74

Traveling back in time

Miles and Directions

0.0 **START** from the gate into Washoe Meadows State Park, and head north on the dirt road. In less than 100 yards, continue straight as a side trail merges from the right. (This is a connector trail to the end of West San Bernardino Avenue.)

0.2 Ignore a series of dirt roads that intersect from the left. Unless you want to explore, stay on the main road and steady your course north up the meadow. Initially the road parallels the Upper Truckee River, with several spur paths leading to it.

1.0 Follow the road as it makes a 90-degree left turn in the middle of the meadow; ignore the singletrack on the right.

1.1 Veer right as the main road turns sharply in front of an old building.

1.2 Turn left at the fork onto a doubletrack through the split-rail fence. Steer clear of the road to the right, which leads to private property.

1.5 Cross the first of two raised boardwalks.

1.6 Just past the second bridge there is a fork in the trail; veer to the right singletrack. (**FYI:** The left trail takes you out of the meadow.) With the extensive tree-clearing in this area, there may be changes in service roads and trails. If the route changes, watch for tire tracks marking the bicycle thoroughfare.

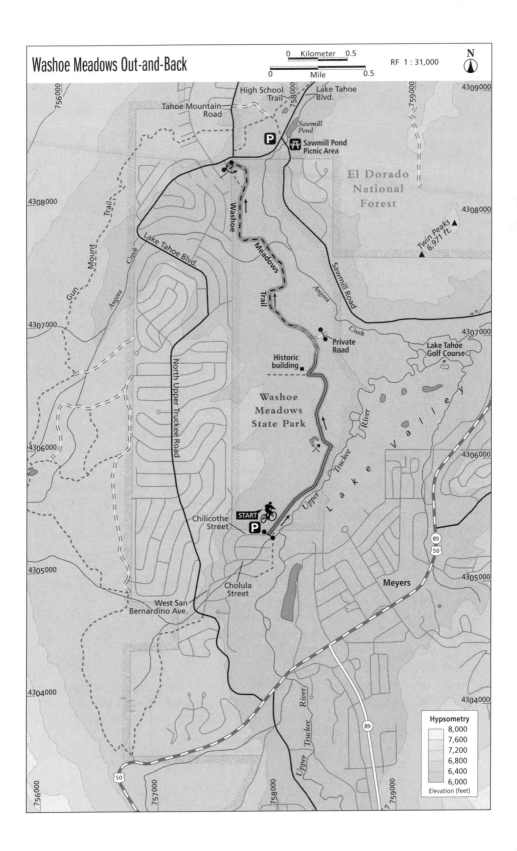

Granite peaks encircling Washoe Meadows

1.8 The trail turns into a service road through a clearing. After 100 yards, turn right away from the road to follow the singletrack. If things have not dried out, it will be marshy up ahead. The trail may split to cross a rivulet; take the left route. The trails will reconnect shortly.

2.1 Cross a fading dual track and come to a vague fork in the trail. Veer right on the well-traveled trail.

2.3 Veer right at the fork on a short section of dual track. You will see some houses on the left; the left trail will take you to the same end point but by a sandier route.

2.6 Reach the gate at the north end of the park. Turn around and retrace your tracks.

5.2 Unless you did some exploring on the return, arrive back where you started.

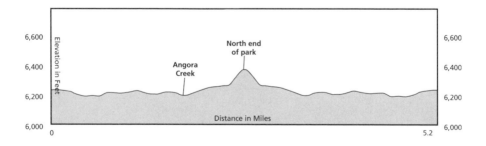

26 Gun Mount Loop

In the land of gonzo climbs, enjoy a tempered cruise through the forest at the base of Angora Ridge and Echo Peak. The narrow Gun Mount Trail weaves behind the Tahoe Paradise neighborhood, with enough curves and obstacles to keep your attention. Briefly emerging from the forest, the trail runs along the escarpment below Flagpole Peak and offers a dramatic view up the cliffs. The turnaround point is the gun mount for avalanche control on U.S. Highway 50 at Meyers Grade. Wait until summer before hitting this trail to let the water subside for the creek crossings. Similarly, if you hold off until mid-July, you can return through Washoe Meadows and miss the road ride.

Start: From the intersection of Sawmill Road and Lake Tahoe Boulevard, South Lake Tahoe
Distance: 10.1-mile loop
Approximate riding time: 1½ hours
Difficulty rating: Moderate—rocks, stream crossings, and modest climbs
Trail surface: 70 percent singletrack, 25 percent paved road, and 5 percent dirt road
Seasons: Late June through October
Other trail users: Hikers
Land status: Lake Tahoe Basin Management Unit

Nearest town: South Lake Tahoe, California
Fees and permits: No fees or permits required
Schedule: 24 hours a day
Maps: Maptech CD: California, High Sierra/Tahoe; USGS maps: Emerald Bay, CA; Echo Lake, CA; Lake Tahoe Trail Map, Adventure Maps, Inc., 2005
Trail contacts: Lake Tahoe Basin Management Unit, USDA Forest Service, 35 College Drive, South Lake Tahoe, CA 96150; (530) 543-2600; www.fs.fed.us/r5/ltbmu

Finding the trailhead: From South Lake Tahoe, drive 2 miles southwest on Lake Tahoe Boulevard from its intersection with California Highway 89 at the Y. The ride begins from the roadside parking area on Lake Tahoe Boulevard at the intersection of Sawmill Pond. There are restrooms across the road at Sawmill Pond. **Trailhead GPS:** N 38 53.32, W 120 01.63

　　Riding from South Lake Tahoe: Head southwest on Lake Tahoe Boulevard 0.6 mile from its intersection with CA 89 at the Y. Catch the singletrack behind the SOUTH LAKE TAHOE HIGH SCHOOL sign on the corner of Viking Road. This pleasant trail parallels the road for 1.4 miles before picking up the directions at Mile 0.1.

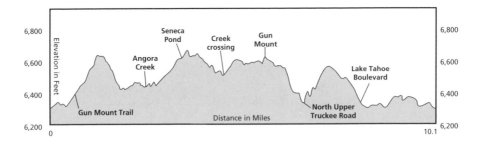

Looking up from the Gun Mount Trail

Miles and Directions

0.0 **START** from the trail in the middle of the log-rail fence at the parking area.

0.1 Turn left at the dirt road and then left again in 100 feet onto the singletrack path between the rocks.

0.4 Ride past the gate, and turn right onto Tahoe Mountain Road.

0.6 Turn left onto the unsigned Gun Mount Trail. Follow the well-traveled path throughout this ride, ignoring the side paths and fading jeep roads.

0.8 Cross the paved road, picking up the singletrack to the left of the power pole for a winding ride into the woods.

2.5 Veer right on the main singletrack. The crossing of Angora Creek is up ahead. (**Bailout:** A left turn on any of the side trails eventually takes you to North Upper Truckee Road.)

3.2 Veer right as a trail merges from the left.

3.5 Arrive at Seneca Pond, aka Hippy Pond. Veer right around the end of the pond before heading back into the forest.

4.0 There are more spur trails on the left that take you into the neighborhood; ignore them all.

4.6 When you see a cabin up ahead, turn right at the fork and cross the creek.

5.1 Veer right at the fork, bypassing the gate on the left. You will soon be riding along the rocky base of Flagpole Peak.

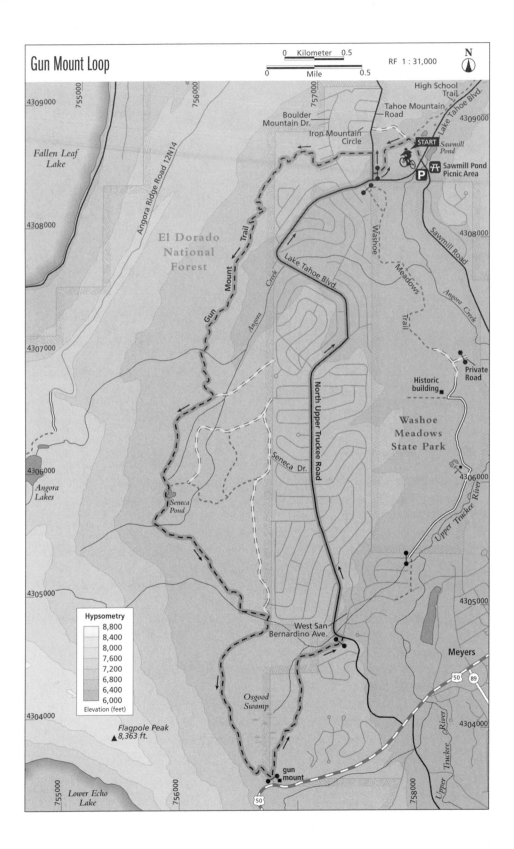

Gun Mount Loop

0 Kilometer 0.5
0 Mile 0.5

RF 1 : 31,000

N

4309000

755000

756000

757000

High School Trail

Tahoe Mountain Road

Boulder Mountain Dr.

Iron Mountain Circle

Lake Tahoe Blvd.

START

Sawmill Pond

P

Sawmill Pond Picnic Area

Sawmill Road

Fallen Leaf Lake

4308000

Angora Ridge Road 12N14

El Dorado National Forest

Gun Mount Trail

Washoe

Meadows Trail

Angora Creek

4307000

Angora Creek

Private Road

Historic building

Washoe Meadows State Park

North Upper Truckee Road

Seneca Dr.

4306000

Angora Lakes

Seneca Pond

Upper Truckee River

4305000

Hypsometry

	8,800
	8,400
	8,000
	7,600
	7,200
	6,800
	6,400
	6,000

Elevation (feet)

West San Bernardino Ave.

Meyers

50 89

4304000

Osgood Swamp

Upper Truckee River

Flagpole Peak
▲ 8,363 ft.

gun mount

50

755000

756000

758000

Lower Echo Lake

Meditation pool along the Gun Mount Trail

5.8 Turn left at the T junction below the gate to the gun mount. (**Option:** This is a good place to turn around for an out-and-back.)

6.0 Veer right at the fork leading to Osgood Swamp on the left.

6.3 Continue straight as a trail merges from the right.

6.7 Drop onto the pavement and turn left onto North Upper Truckee Road. (**Option:** If it's July and the meadows are dry, ride straight onto West San Bernardino Avenue. Take the dirt trail at the end of the road into Washoe Meadows State Park. Weave your way north through the park and back to Lake Tahoe Boulevard.)

8.3 Turn left at Lake Tahoe Boulevard, following the yellow stripe.

9.6 Turn left onto Tahoe Mountain Road to complete the loop. Make a quick right turn to ride around the gate and retrace your tracks.

10.0 Turn right onto the dirt road and then right on the singletrack back to the start.

10.1 Arrive back at the parking area.

27 Upper Truckee River Out-and-Back

This ride is an easy meander along the peaceful Upper Truckee River. Enjoy narrow paths through grassy meadows near the river's edge and forested trails along the upper banks. Wildflowers and views of the surrounding peaks add to the flavor of this short trek. The ride starts next to the site of the weekend Tahoe Flea Market and ends across the river from the Lake Tahoe Airport. There are many side trails to the river and adjoining neighborhood along the way. Wear your swimsuit on this ride, and take a dip when the weather's warm.

Just beyond the turnaround point is a maze of trails between the Upper Truckee River and Pioneer Trail. The locals have their own routes through this undeveloped slice of national forest. Explore these trails with a local guide or a keen sense of adventure.

Start: From the east side of the Elks Lodge off U.S. Highway 50, South Lake Tahoe

Distance: 4.6-mile out-and-back

Approximate riding time: 30 to 45 minutes

Difficulty rating: Easy—flat and nontechnical ride, although after 1.5 miles there are some nasty hike-a-bike sections, dips, and slippery slopes

Trail surface: Singletrack

Seasons: July through October

Other trail users: Hikers and dogs

Land status: Lake Tahoe Basin Management Unit

Nearest town: South Lake Tahoe, California

Fees and permits: No fees or permits required

Schedule: 24 hours a day

Maps: Maptech CD: California, High Sierra/Tahoe; USGS maps: South Lake Tahoe, CA, Emerald Bay, CA; Echo Lake, CA

Trail contact: Lake Tahoe Basin Management Unit, USDA Forest Service, 35 College Drive, South Lake Tahoe, CA 96150; (530) 543-2600; www.fs.fed.us/r5/ltbmu

Finding the trailhead: From South Lake Tahoe, drive south 2.8 miles on US 50 from its intersection with California Highway 89 at the Y. Just past the Upper Truckee River, turn left onto Elks Club Road. The ride begins on the left at the gate and dirt road just past the Elks Lodge. On Sunday and some Saturdays, the Tahoe Flea Market is under way next to the trailhead from 8:00 A.M. to 5:00 P.M. **Trailhead GPS:** N 38 52.49, W 120 00.20

Miles and Directions

0.0 **START** from the gate and follow the dual track. When the flea market is under way, this means climbing over the string of flags and a NO PARKING sign in front of the gate.

0.1 Slip under the metal fence. Just beyond is a dirt road on the right—ignore it and continue straight on the dual track.

0.3 The trail narrows through the meadow and follows the river hidden behind the brush. There are many side trails on the left that will take you to the river's edge. If you miss the main thoroughfare and come to the river—oh well. Enjoy and backtrack when you are ready.

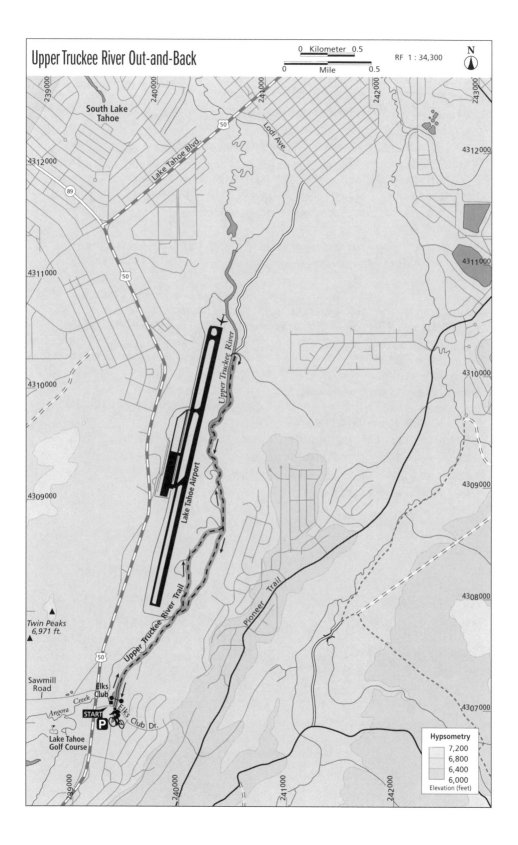

Upper Truckee River Out-and-Back

0   Kilometer   0.5

0   Mile   0.5

RF 1 : 34,300

N

South Lake
Tahoe

Lake Tahoe Blvd.

Lodi Ave.

Upper Truckee River

Lake Tahoe Airport

Upper Truckee River Trail

Pioneer Trail

Twin Peaks
6,971 ft.

Sawmill
Road

Elks
Club

Angora Creek

START

Elks Club Dr.

Lake Tahoe
Golf Course

Hypsometry

| 7,200 |
| 6,800 |
| 6,400 |
| 6,000 |

Elevation (feet)

0.6 Veer left at the fork to follow the river. You will return to this point from the right to complete a loop.

1.0 Veer right at the fork, and cross through the meadow.

1.2 Turn left at the T intersection to follow the river downstream. (**Bailout:** Turn right, and loop back to the start.)

1.3 Veer right at the fork, where the left path goes along the riverbank.

1.5 Continue straight where a series of neighborhood trails join from right. There will soon be some hike-a-bike sections up a steep bank and over tree roots. Beginners or young children may want to turn around at this point.

1.6 Keep straight as you cross more neighborhood trails leading to the river. Watch out for a massive dip in the trail.

2.0 Take either path where the trail splits at the property boundary sign for the national forest land. The left trail gets close and personal with the river. The trails connect in 50 yards.

2.3 The trail drops onto the paved road leading across the river to the airport. This is the turnaround point; head back along the river. (**Option:** Turn right onto the paved road. By going straight at all the junctions and passing through the South Tahoe Public Utility District (STPUD) gates, you will come to a residential neighborhood in a little over a mile. There will be plenty of side trails to explore along the way. Once you reach the neighborhood, continue straight to Lodi Avenue. A left turn will take you into South Lake Tahoe.)

3.4 Continue straight through two trail intersections: First, bypass the trail on the right, and then veer right as a trail comes in from the left. (**Option:** Turn right at the first intersection to retrace your path along the river.)

3.7 Veer right as a trail merges from the left. Head up the rise into the woods.

3.8 Veer right for a gentler ride through the trees.

4.0 Turn left at the T intersection, completing the loop.

4.6 Arrive back at the Elks Club.

28 Angora Lakes Out-and-Back

Warm up with a bit of singletrack along Fallen Leaf Road before the long, steady climb up Angora Ridge. A lookout on the ridge offers dramatic views of Fallen Leaf Lake, Mount Tallac, and Lake Tahoe on one side and the Upper Truckee River Basin on the other. Don't be misled, you can drive nearly all the way on the narrow, rough, and mostly dirt road. There is a surprisingly large parking lot at the end of the road before the last trail run up to the lakes. The glacial Angora Lakes back up against steep granite cliffs below Angora Peak and the Desolation Wilderness. The upper lake is bordered by a small lodge, cabins, and a beach that offers swimming, rowing, cliff jumping, and fishing. This is a popular spot, with a fair amount of vehicle traffic on weekends. Watch for cars, particularly on the downhill run.

Start: From Fallen Leaf Road, 0.25 mile south of Fallen Leaf Campground
Distance: 10.1-mile out-and-back
Approximate riding time: 1½ to 2 hours
Difficulty rating: Moderate—nontechnical; long, steady climb
Trail surface: 42 percent dirt road, 38 percent singletrack, and 20 percent paved road
Seasons: Late May through October
Other trail users: Hikers, equestrians, and vehicles

Land status: Lake Tahoe Basin Management Unit
Nearest town: South Lake Tahoe, California
Fees and permits: No fees or permits required
Schedule: 24 hours a day
Maps: Maptech CD: California, High Sierra/Tahoe; USGS maps: Emerald Bay, CA; Echo Lake, CA
Trail contact: Lake Tahoe Basin Management Unit, USDA Forest Service, 35 College Drive, South Lake Tahoe, CA 96150; (530) 543-2600; www.fs.fed.us/r5/ltbmu

Finding the trailhead: From South Lake Tahoe, drive north on California Highway 89 for 3 miles from the Y intersection with U.S. Highway 50. Turn left onto Fallen Leaf Road; this is across from the entrance to the Tallac Historic Site. The trailhead is on the left (east side of the road) 0.8 mile down Fallen Leaf Road, just beyond the campground. There are small parking areas on both sides of the road. Water and restrooms are at the campground. **Trailhead GPS:** N 38 55.36, W 120 02.73

Miles and Directions

0.0 START from the gate to Forest Road 12N19. In 100 feet, turn right at the fork onto the unsigned, narrow Parallel Trail. The trail starts out sandy and rather chewed up by horses.

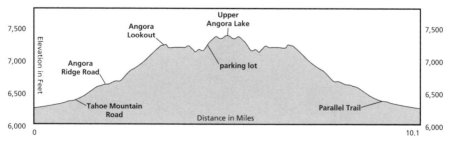

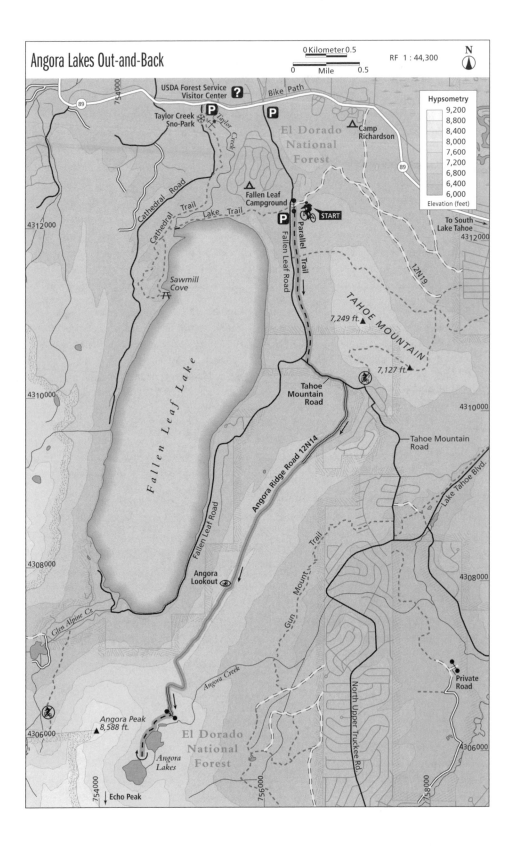

Angora Lakes Out-and-Back

0 Kilometer 0.5

0 Mile 0.5

RF 1 : 44,300

N

USDA Forest Service
Visitor Center ?   Bike Path

Taylor Creek
Sno-Park

Taylor Creek

89

754000

El Dorado
National
Forest

Camp
Richardson

89

P

Fallen Leaf
Campground

Cathedral Road

Cathedral   Trail

Lake   Trail

4312000

Fallen Leaf Road

P   Parallel Trail

START

To South
Lake Tahoe

4312000

12N19

Sawmill
Cove

7,249 ft.

TAHOE MOUNTAIN

7,127 ft.

4310000

Fallen Leaf Lake

Tahoe
Mountain
Road

4310000

Tahoe Mountain
Road

Angora Ridge Road 12N14

Lake Tahoe Blvd.

4308000

Fallen Leaf Road

Angora
Lookout

Gun   Mount.   Trail

4308000

Glen Alpine Cr.

Angora Creek

North Upper Truckee Rd.

Private
Road

4306000

Angora Peak
8,588 ft.

El Dorado
National
Forest

4306000

754000

Angora
Lakes

756000

758000

Echo Peak

Hypsometry

9,200
8,800
8,400
8,000
7,600
7,200
6,800
6,400
6,000

Elevation (feet)

1.2 Turn left and climb up the paved Tahoe Mountain Road.

1.5 Turn right on the unsigned and unpaved road with the bicycle SHARE THE ROAD sign. This is Angora Ridge Road, Forest Road 12N14.

3.3 Arrive at Angora Lookout and a spanning view.

4.3 Ride through the parking lot to the gate at the far end. Follow the unpaved service road up to the lake. This is where trucks ferry guests to their cabins.

4.8 Turn right at the fork, pass the lower lake, and head to the upper lake.

5.0 Reach the buildings and end of the trail for bikes. Park your steed in the rack with the provided locks. Try the famed lemonade, and enjoy the lake before heading down the mountain.

5.7 Return through the parking lot and down the road.

8.6 Turn left at Tahoe Mountain Road.

8.9 Turn right back onto Parallel Trail.

10.1 Arrive back at the starting point.

29 Fallen Leaf Lake Loop

Meander through mixed forests of pine and aspen around Fallen Leaf Lake and along Taylor Creek. While the trail itself reaches the shore in only a few places, there are plenty of spur trails that take you to the water's edge. The view across the lake to the granite mountains beyond is postcard perfect. Once you head away from the lake, you truly enter the woods as the trail narrows and twists tightly through the trees. Many of the trails follow the winter cross-country ski routes of the Taylor Creek Sno-Park, an alternate starting point for this double loop. Yes, there is a maze of trails through these woods—none of which are signed. If you get off track, you will eventually come to the lake, Taylor Creek, or Cathedral Road, unless you are going in circles. This is a beautiful place to get lost.

Start: From Fallen Leaf Road, 0.25 mile south of Fallen Leaf Campground
Distance: 4.9-mile loop
Approximate riding time: 45 minutes
Difficulty rating: Easy—mostly flat and nontechnical
Trail surface: 70 percent singletrack, 21 percent paved road, and 9 percent paved bike path
Seasons: June through October
Other trail users: Hikers, equestrians, and vehicles

Land status: Lake Tahoe Basin Management Unit
Nearest town: South Lake Tahoe, California
Fees and permits: No fees or permits required
Schedule: 24 hours a day
Maps: Maptech CD: California, High Sierra/Tahoe; USGS map: Emerald Bay, CA
Trail contact: Lake Tahoe Basin Management Unit, USDA Forest Service, 35 College Drive, South Lake Tahoe, CA 96150; (530) 543-2600; www.fs.fed.us/r5/ltbmu

Touching the edge of Fallen Leaf Lake

Finding the trailhead: From South Lake Tahoe, drive 3 miles north on California Highway 89 from the Y intersection with U.S. Highway 50. Turn left onto Fallen Leaf Road, which is across from the entrance to the Tallac Historic Site. The trailhead is on the right (west side of the road) 0.8 mile down Fallen Leaf Road, just past the campground. There are small parking areas on both sides of the road. Water and restrooms are at the campground. **Trailhead GPS:** N 38 55.35, W 120 02.75

Miles and Directions

0.0 **START** at the trail on the west side of the road, just south of the parking area. Follow the sign and arrow to Fallen Leaf Lake.

0.2 Turn right at the intersection of trails. Make a quick left turn around some boulders. Ignore the side trails; you are working your way to the main access road from the campground to the lake. (**Option:** Continue straight at the intersection for a short hike-a-bike over the berm separating the campground from the lake. From the top, turn right to ride counterclockwise around the lake.)

0.3 Veer left at the fork.

0.4 Cross the dirt road connecting the campground to the lake, and continue straight on a main path. Ignore the side trails merging from the left, and ride counterclockwise around the lake. For the best view of the lake, take one of the spur trails to the lake's edge.

Fallen Leaf Lake Loop

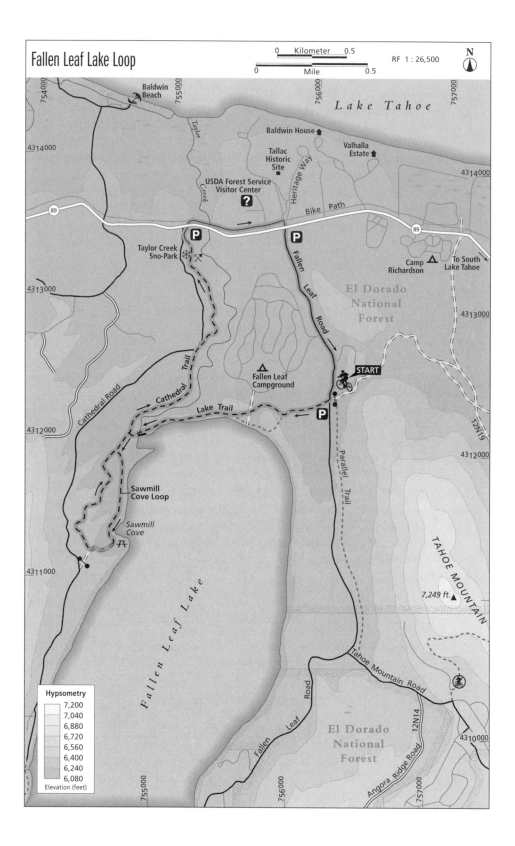

0   Kilometer   0.5

0   Mile   0.5

RF 1 : 26,500

N

Baldwin Beach

Lake Tahoe

Baldwin House

Taylor Creek

Tallac Historic Site

Valhalla Estate

USDA Forest Service Visitor Center

?

89

Bike Path

89

Taylor Creek Sno-Park

P

P

Fallen Leaf Road

Camp Richardson

To South Lake Tahoe

El Dorado National Forest

4314000

4314000

4313000

4313000

Cathedral Trail

Fallen Leaf Campground

START

Cathedral Road

Lake Trail

P

12N19

4312000

4312000

Sawmill Cove Loop

Parallel Trail

Sawmill Cove

Fallen Leaf Lake

TAHOE MOUNTAIN

4311000

7,249 ft.

Tahoe Mountain Road

Fallen Leaf Road

12N14

Angora Ridge Road

El Dorado National Forest

4310000

Hypsometry

7,200
7,040
6,880
6,720
6,560
6,400
6,240
6,080
Elevation (feet)

754000   755000   756000   757000

0.9 Ride straight through the intersection of trails to cross over the lake's narrow spillway. Once on the other side, continue straight to a T intersection with a wider path cutting through a large log on the right. Turn left here.

1.1 Veer left at the fork. You will return to this spot from the right to complete the Sawmill Cove Loop. Again, ignore the spur trails that cut over to the lake. There will be a short climb up ahead.

1.5 At the picnic table on Sawmill Cove, veer right on the dirt road. Pass an old foundation on the left; the tempting trail on the left doesn't go very far.

1.7 Turn right onto a doubletrack leading around a garage and cabin. The trail soon fades into a singletrack.

1.9 Continue straight as a trail merges from the right. Follow the blue diamond markers for the cross-country ski route. You are truly in the woods as the trail weaves through the trees.

2.1 Turn right at the T intersection onto a wider trail.

2.3 Veer left at the fork, completing the Sawmill Cove Loop. This time, continue straight where the trail passes through the cut log. (**Option:** Turn right before the log, and return back to the start.)

2.4 Ride straight up the hill and over the water bars. At the top, veer right at the fork to ride along the ledge above Taylor Creek. Ignore the spur trails to the creek on the right.

2.8 Continue straight where a trail merges from the left and head toward the split-rail fence and paved road. Ignore the side trails along the way.

2.9 Pass through the fence and, as you near the road, veer right to stay on the singletrack. You will follow the blue diamond markers again. (**Option:** Ride the paved Cathedral Road to the bike path along CA 89.)

3.4 Turn left, up, and over the berm for a steep drop into the parking lot. Ride through the lot for the Taylor Creek Sno-Park, and turn right on the unsigned Cathedral Road.

3.6 Carefully cross CA 89 and turn right on the paved bike path.

4.0 Cross the road to the USDA Forest Service Visitor Center. (**Side trip:** Turn left and visit.)

4.1 Turn right for a brief ride on Heritage Way. Immediately cross back over CA 89 and ride along Fallen Leaf Road. (**Side trip:** Turn left on Heritage Way, and explore the Tallac Historic Site and Beach.)

4.9 Arrive back at the trailhead.

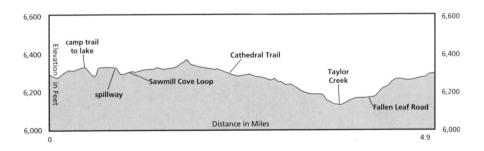

Truckee

The Truckee area is just north of the Lake Tahoe Basin and has been broadly applied to what's within easy striking distance from the town of Truckee and over the ridge from the North Shore of Lake Tahoe. New trails and the mountain bike park at Northstar at Tahoe are making this a biking destination in its own right. The ever popular Hole-in-the-Ground Trail starts at Donner Pass and will one day be accessible to Truckee via the Donner Lake Rim Trail.

Yes, the exciting news out of Truckee is the emerging Donner Lake Rim Trail. Construction is under way for this 23.0-mile multiuse trail that will eventually follow the ridges surrounding Donner Lake. In time, this will provide legitimate access to the Schallenberger Ridge south of the lake. Keep an eye on this trail, and keep in mind that your financial support and helping hands will help make this happen sooner than later.

Truckee and the reservoirs northeast of town sit a little lower than Lake Tahoe, offering some of the first riding of the season. The ride to Verde Peak has been included to offer a literal overview of the Stampede and Boca Reservoirs. While this guide stops at Stampede Reservoir (the line has to stop somewhere), there are numerous Forest Service roads beyond in the Sardine Valley.

There is more to ride in Truckee, but public access has prevented these trails from being included here. With a little conversation at the local bike shops, you can get the update on these additional rides. This is your start—now fan out.

30 Sawtooth Ridge Trail Loop

Perched on a broad terrace overlooking the Truckee River, this ride is flat by Tahoe standards. There are several precipitous overlooks along the way that offer fine views of Tinker Knob and Squaw Peak to the west. With endless twists and turns, this trail covers lots of miles in a relatively small area. Limitless loose and jagged rocks will keep you focused on the trail. If the rocks and sharp turns become unnerving, there are several opportunities to bail and ride the dirt road back to the parking lot. For a longer ride, you can continue on Forest Service Route 06 toward the top of Northstar-at-Tahoe ski area or on to Tahoe City.

Start: From the trailhead to Sawtooth Ridge Trail

Distance: 11.2-mile loop

Approximate riding time: 1.5 to 2 hours

Difficulty rating: Moderate—lots of rocks, tight turns, and a short climb

Trail surface: Singletrack

Seasons: Late May to November

Other trail users: Hikers, joggers, and dogs

Land status: Tahoe National Forest

Nearest town: Truckee, California

Fees and permits: No fees or permits required

Schedule: 24 hours a day

Maps: Maptech CD: California, High Sierra/Tahoe; USGS map: Truckee, CA; Lake Tahoe Trail Map, Adventure Maps, Inc., 2005

Trail contact: Tahoe National Forest, USDA Forest Service, Truckee Ranger District, 9646 Donner Pass Road, Truckee, CA 96161; (530) 587-3558; www.fs.fed.us/r5/tahoe

Finding the trailhead: Drive east from historic Truckee on Donner Pass Road. Turn right onto Brockway Road and then right again on Palisades Road, which turns into Ponderosa Drive. Turn right onto Silver Fir Drive and left onto Thelin Drive. Take the first dirt road on the right; this gated entrance is to FSR 06. The trailhead is up ahead at the parking lot on the right. There is no water or restroom at the trailhead. **Trailhead GPS:** N 39 18.3, W 120 11.3

Miles and Directions

0.0 **START** on the singletrack at the information board.

0.3 Cross the dirt road. This is the first of many road crossings; at each crossing, pick up the singletrack on the other side.

1.1 Trail nears the edge of the terrace for a dramatic view of the Truckee River below.

2.0 Veer right, staying on Sawtooth Ridge Trail. You will complete the loop portion of the ride at this point.

3.4 Turn right for a side-trip loop to an overlook. Go either way around the loop. (**Option:** Continue straight if you must, shaving off 0.4 mile.)

3.8 Return to the main trail, and turn right.

Overlooking the Truckee River from Sawtooth Ridge Trail ▶

Cutting along the Sawtooth Ridge Trail

5.2 Cross FSR 06 and pass in front of another information board. (**Option:** Turn right and head up toward Mount Watson. At the intersection with Forest Service Road 73, a right turn will take you into Tahoe City.)

5.4 Pass over another dirt road.

6.1 Cross a dirt road.

6.3 Cross a dirt road.

6.6 Turn left at the T intersection with a dirt road, following the SAWTOOTH TRAIL sign.

6.7 Turn right onto the singletrack posted with a NO MOTORIZED BIKES sign.

7.3 Cross over a dirt road before beginning the climb.

9.2 Cross FSR 06 again. Ride past the information board, and turn right to head back toward the parking lot. This completes the loop portion of the ride.

11.2 Arrive back to the parking lot.

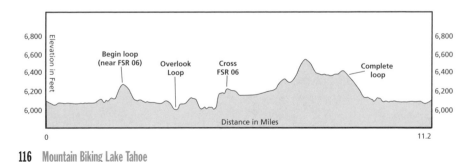

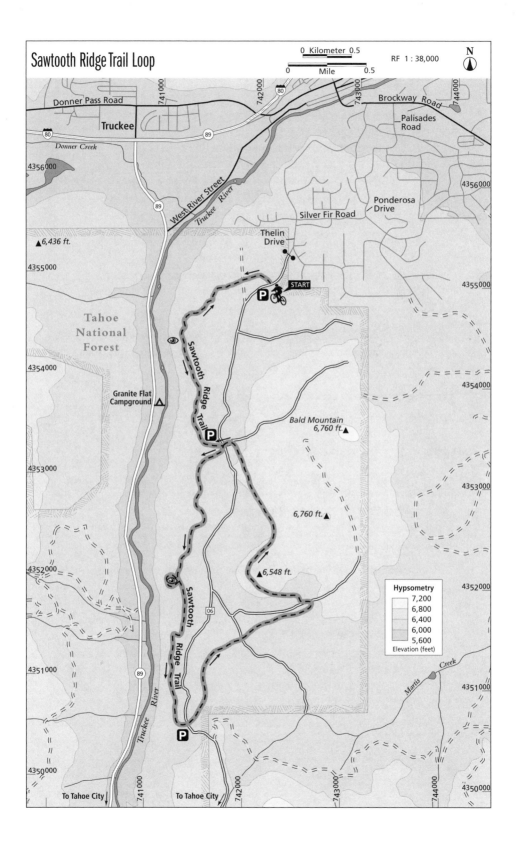

Sawtooth Ridge Trail Loop

0 Kilometer 0.5
0 Mile 0.5

RF 1 : 38,000

N

Donner Pass Road

741000

742000

80

743000

Brockway Road

744000

Truckee

89

Palisades Road

80

West River Street

Donner Creek

Truckee River

4356000

4356000

Silver Fir Road

Ponderosa Drive

Thelin Drive

▲6,436 ft.

4355000

START

P

4355000

Tahoe National Forest

Sawtooth Ridge Trail

4354000

4354000

Granite Flat Campground ⛺

P

Bald Mountain 6,760 ft. ▲

4353000

4353000

6,760 ft. ▲

4352000

▲6,548 ft.

4352000

Hypsometry
7,200
6,800
6,400
6,000
5,600
Elevation (feet)

Sawtooth Ridge Trail

06

4351000

89

Sawtooth Ridge Trail

Martis Creek

4351000

Truckee River

P

4350000

4350000

To Tahoe City

741000

To Tahoe City

742000

743000

744000

31 Emigrant Trail to Stampede Reservoir Out-and-Back

Take a journey back in time and follow the spirit of the early settlers. This popular and well-marked trail parallels the actual pathway the pioneers traveled on their westward migration. Unlike the course of the emigrants, this is a smooth, well-worn path for beginner and intermediate riders. There are a few mini rock gardens and plenty of nice curves, gentle climbs, and some smooth downhill cruising. While this is an easy ride, it is not flat; the climbs are gradual and short. Most of the ride is through an open forest, with nice views of the peaks and reservoirs along the way. This is one of the first trails to dry out in spring. Go as far as you want.

Start: From Donner Camp Picnic Ground on California Highway 89
Distance: 22.6-mile out-and-back
Approximate riding time: 3 hours
Difficulty rating: Easy to moderate—relatively flat and nontechnical; moderate for the full distance and grade
Trail surface: Singletrack
Seasons: May through October
Other trail users: Hikers, joggers, and equestrians
Land status: Tahoe National Forest

Nearest town: Truckee, California
Fees and permits: No fees or permits required
Schedule: 24 hours a day
Maps: Maptech CD: California, High Sierra/Tahoe; USGS maps: Truckee, CA; Hobart Mills, CA
Trail contact: Tahoe National Forest, USDA Forest Service, Truckee Ranger District, 9646 Donner Pass Road, Truckee, CA 96161; (530) 587-3558; www.fs.fed.us/r5/tahoe

Finding the trailhead: From Truckee, take U.S. Highway 80 east and exit on CA 89 North. Drive nearly 3 miles north to the Donner Camp Picnic Ground on the right. There is a restroom but no water. **Trailhead GPS:** N 39 22.55, W 120 10.87

Miles and Directions

0.0 **START** at the trailhead to the Commemorative Emigrant Trail, to the left of the self-guided loop for hikers only.

0.4 Pass over the first of many dirt roads along this ride. Unless noted otherwise, simply cross these roads and follow the well-trodden singletrack on the other side. The trail is well signed; any turns will be marked.

1.0 Cross the paved road leading to Prosser Creek Reservoir and the campgrounds; the singletrack veers down to the left.

1.3 Continue straight through a series of intersections with dirt roads and trails for the campground.

1.8 Cross over a dirt road.

Smooth line to Stampede Lake ▶

Not exactly the path the settlers followed

1.9 Turn left at the fork, following the HIGHWAY 89 BRIDGE CROSSING sign. (**Shortcut:** When the river is low, take the right fork. If you are sure the creek is passable, charge across. Turn right when you connect with the Emigrant Trail on the other side, just beyond Mile 3.3 below.)

2.6 Ride up to CA 89, turn right, and cross Prosser Creek along the road. At the end of the bridge, turn right into the parking area and pick up the singletrack at the information board.

3.3 Veer right onto the road for about 50 yards, then veer left uphill on the singletrack.

3.6 Cross another paved road leading to Prosser Creek Reservoir.

4.5 Pass over a dirt road.

5.7 Pass over another dirt road.

6.5 Arrive at the top of a ridge. This is a good turnaround spot if you aren't going the whole way.

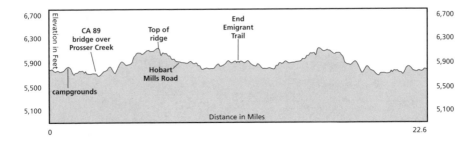

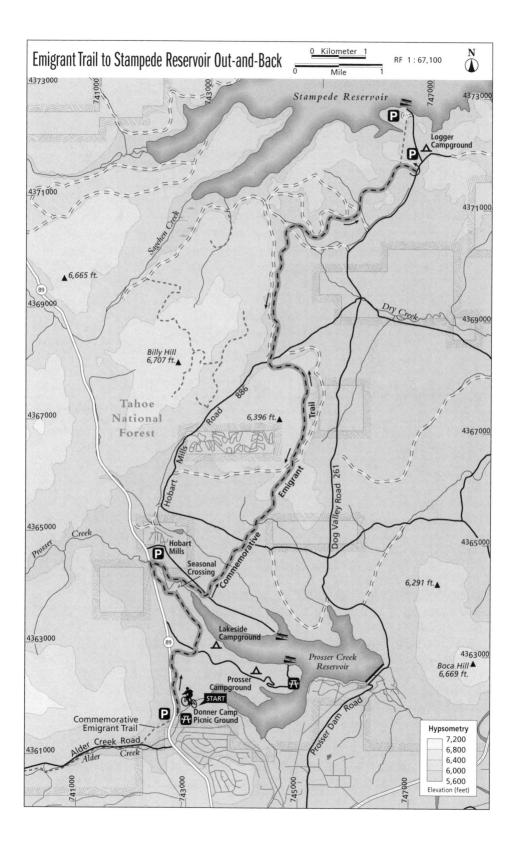

Emigrant Trail to Stampede Reservoir Out-and-Back

RF 1 : 67,100

0 ___ Kilometer ___ 1

0 ___ Mile ___ 1

N

Stampede Reservoir

Logger Campground

Saghen Creek

Dry Creek

▲ 6,665 ft.

89

Billy Hill
6,707 ft.▲

Tahoe
National
Forest

886

Road

Hobart

Mills

6,396 ft.▲

Emigrant

Trail

Commemorative

Dog Valley Road 261

6,291 ft.▲

Hobart
Mills

Seasonal
Crossing

Prosser

Creek

Lakeside
Campground

*Prosser Creek
Reservoir*

Boca Hill ▲
6,669 ft.

89

Prosser
Campground

Commemorative
Emigrant Trail

START

Donner Camp
Picnic Ground

Alder Creek Road

Alder   Creek

Prosser Dam Road

Hypsometry	
	7,200
	6,800
	6,400
	6,000
	5,600
Elevation (feet)	

6.7	Cross the dirt road and cruise the downhill.
7.3	Cross the paved road, picking up the singletrack on the other side—not the dirt road.
7.8	Cross the dirt road, and drop down steeply.
10.2	Cross a gravel road.
10.9	Pass over two parallel dirt roads.
11.0	Veer right at the fork to Captain Roberts Boat Ramp. (**Option:** Turn left and head toward Stampede Reservoir. If the water level is high, part of the trail may be unrideable. The trail approaches the water's edge, crosses an inlet, and continues up to a parking lot. Ride across the parking lot and catch the singletrack to the launch ramp. This is 0.9 mile; there is a restroom and water here but no food.)
11.2	Cross the dirt road. Stampede Reservoir appears in the distance on the left.
11.3	Reach the end of the Emigrant Trail and turnaround point. The return will go faster as you retrace your tracks. (**Option:** If you want to ride down to the lake, turn left onto the paved Dog Valley Road and left again at the intersection. You will finish up at Captain Roberts Boat Ramp.)
22.6	Arrive back at the Donner Camp Picnic Ground. (**Option:** For a longer ride, cross CA 89 and continue on the Emigrant Trail to the Alder Creek trailhead.)

32 Emigrant Trail to Alder Creek Out-and-Back

It's hard to imagine wagons moving through Alder Creek Canyon or, worse yet, holding up for a winter here. Hold that thought as you take an easy cruise along Alder Creek—that's not a smooth easy. While the trail is well traveled and hard packed, there are enough rocks to keep you focused. Eight stream crossings mean waiting until the creeks subside in early summer before offering yourself to the mosquitoes along here. Follow the trail downstream for a couple of miles, then cut through the forest until you reach California Highway 89 at the Donner Camp Picnic Ground. From there the trail continues all the way to Stampede Lake. Go as far as you like.

Start: From the Alder Creek trailhead to the Emigrant Trail
Distance: 6.4-mile out-and-back
Approximate riding time: 1 hour
Difficulty rating: Easy—nonstrenuous ride with rocks and stream crossings
Trail surface: Singletrack
Seasons: July through October
Other trail users: Hikers and equestrians
Land status: Tahoe National Forest

Nearest town: Truckee, California
Fees and permits: No fees or permits required
Schedule: 24 hours a day
Maps: Maptech CD: California, High Sierra/Tahoe; USGS map: Truckee, CA
Trail contact: Tahoe National Forest, USDA Forest Service, Truckee Ranger District, 9646 Donner Pass Road, Truckee, CA 96161; (530) 587-3558; www.fs.fed.us/r5/tahoe

Finding the trailhead: From Truckee, head north on Northwoods Boulevard for about 3.8 miles from Donner Pass Road. Turn right onto Fjord Road and right again onto Alder Creek Road.

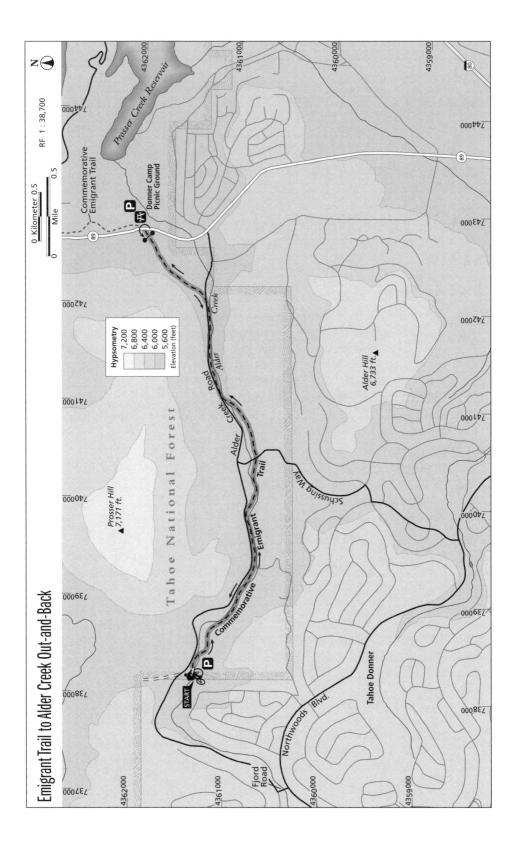

Emigrant Trail to Alder Creek Out-and-Back

N

RF 1 : 38,700

0 Kilometer 0.5

0 Mile 0.5

Hypsometry
7,200
6,800
6,400
6,000
5,600
Elevation (feet)

Prosser Creek Reservoir

Commemorative
Emigrant Trail

P

Donner Camp
Picnic Ground

89

Tahoe National Forest

Prosser Hill
▲ 7,171 ft.

Alder Creek Road

Alder Creek

Emigrant Trail

Commemorative

Alder Hill
6,733 ft. ▲

Schussing Way

START

P

Fiord Road

Northwoods Blvd.

Tahoe Donner

80

88

4362000
4361000
4360000
4359000

737000
738000
739000
740000
741000
742000
743000
744000

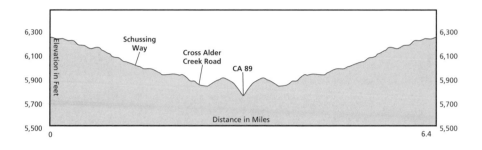

Drive 1.7 miles to where Alder Creek Road crosses a dirt road. The trailhead is just down the dirt road on the right (south side). There is parking off both sides of Alder Creek Road. **Trailhead GPS:** N 39 22.09, W 120 13.68

Miles and Directions

0.0 **START** from the trailhead and information board for the Commemorative Emigrant Trail.

0.2 This is the first of four stream crossings. If it doesn't look fordable, the other crossings don't get any better; remember—you will do them all twice. Soon after you cross the stream, there is a merging of trails. Veer left and head downstream. The trail is well packed, with plenty of rocks; you are riding near the riverbed.

0.7 Time for the second creek crossing.

1.2 Third creek crossing—if you don't want to ride them, there are stepping-stones to balance your way across.

1.3 Cross Schussing Way, which comes from Tahoe Donner on the right.

1.7 Count 'em—fourth river crossing.

2.4 Cross Alder Creek Road, leaving the creek behind, and head into the forest. The trail is well signed on the other side.

2.8 This is the top of the climb, with a short downhill cruise ahead.

3.0 Cross the dirt road, and continue on the singletrack.

3.2 Arrive at the gate and CA 89. Turn around and head back the way you came. (**Option:** Cross the highway into Donner Camp Picnic Ground and continue on the Emigrant Trail toward Prosser Creek and Stampede Reservoir, 11.3 miles from this gate. There are outhouses at the picnic area but no water.)

5.7 Stay to the right as a trail comes in from the left.

6.1 Veer right at the fork, and head for the last stream crossing.

6.4 Arrive back at the trailhead.

33 Donner Lake Rim Trail Out-and-Back

Follow the recently completed section of the Donner Lake Rim Trail (DLRT), an exciting gateway for mountain bikers into the Castle Peak backcountry. This is the beginning of 23 miles of singletrack that will eventually encircle the Donner Lake Basin. Access to the DLRT begins at the bottom of Negro Canyon near U.S. Highway 80. A ragged access trail climbs up to an intersection with the rim trail, a beautiful and well-built singletrack. Once on the DLRT, you can head west through meadows of mule's ear to Summit Lake. When the next section of the rim trail is completed, it will connect with the Hole-in-the-Ground Trail. Heading east on the DLRT, you climb a series of well-graded switchbacks to an overlook on Donner Ridge. In both directions, the lower portions of the trails are exposed through the chaparral, offering incredible views of Mount Lincoln, Donner Lake, and Castle Peak. Even under the cover of the forest near the top of both ridges, the views are stunning.

Start: From Negro Canyon off US 80
Distance: 9.7-mile out-and-back
Approximate riding time: 1½ to 2 hours
Difficulty rating: Moderate—rocky start, steady climb, and switchbacks
Trail surface: 75 percent singletrack, 25 percent dirt road
Seasons: July through October; the eastern section to Donner Ridge is okay in June
Other trail users: Hikers, equestrians, and vehicles
Land status: Tahoe National Forest; Truckee Donner Land Trust
Nearest town: Truckee, California

Fees and permits: No fees or permits required
Schedule: 24 hours a day
Maps: Maptech CD: California, High Sierra/Tahoe; USGS map: Norden, CA
Trail contacts: Tahoe National Forest, USDA Forest Service, Truckee Ranger District, 9646 Donner Pass Road, Truckee, CA 96161; (530) 587-3558; www.fs.fed.us/r5/tahoe.
Truckee Donner Land Trust, P.O. Box 8816, Truckee, CA 96162; (530) 582-4711; www.tdlandtrust.org.
Tahoe Donner Association, 11509 Northwoods Boulevard, Truckee, CA 96161; (503) 587-9400.

Finding the trailhead: From Truckee, drive west on US 80 and take the Donner Lake exit (exit 180), the last off-ramp before reaching Donner Pass. Immediately turn right onto the dirt road

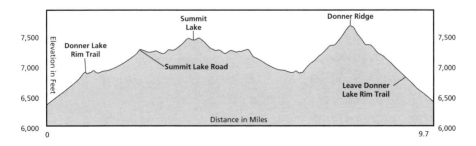

Donner Lake from the new rim trail

signed DONNER LAKE RIM TRAIL. This is the base of Negro Canyon. The trailhead is at the end of the large dirt parking area. There is no water or outhouse. **Trailhead GPS:** N 39 20.01, W 120 17.46

Miles and Directions

0.0   **START** from Donner Lake Rim Trail kiosk, where the road splits at the end of the parking area. The Summit Lake Road heads up the canyon on the left. Take the right overgrown jeep trail, which is no longer accessible to motorized vehicles. The trail begins with a rocky, steep climb.

0.9   Reach the singletrack Donner Lake Rim Trail. Turn left for an out-and-back to Summit Lake. You will return to this spot and do another out-and-back to the right toward Donner Ridge and the Tahoe Donner trail system.

1.1   Turn left on the dirt road. Keep an eye out for the singletrack up ahead on the right.

1.2   Veer right upslope onto the singletrack. Enjoy the view while gaining elevation on the meandering and well-graded trail.

2.3   Veer right at the end of the singletrack, and drop down onto unsigned Summit Lake Road.

3.0   Turn right at the fork.

3.4   Arrive at picturesque Summit Lake. Turn around and retrace your route back to the T junction with the Negro Canyon access trail. (**FYI:** In July 2006 construction will begin on a bike route west of the lake that will connect with the Hole-in-the-Ground Trail.)

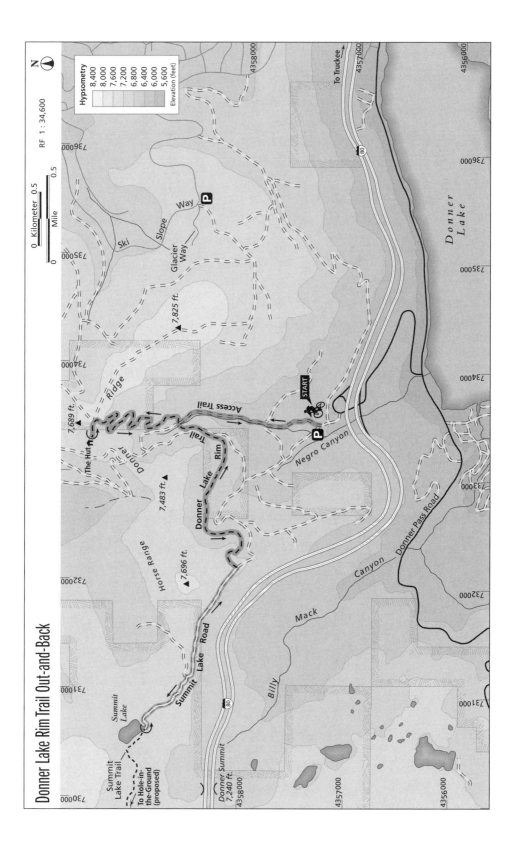

Donner Lake Rim Trail Out-and-Back

N

RF 1 : 34,600

0 Kilometer 0.5

0 Mile 0.5

Hypsometry

8,400
8,000
7,600
7,200
6,800
6,400
6,000
5,600

Elevation (feet)

To Truckee

Donner Lake

80

Ski Slope Way

P

Glacier Way

▲ 7,825 ft.

Ridge

▲ 7,689 ft.

The Hut

Donner Trail

Access Trail

START

Donner Lake Rim Trail

P

Negro Canyon

▲ 7,483 ft.

Horse Range

▲ 7,696 ft.

Summit Lake Road

Mack Canyon

Billy Canyon

Donner Pass Road

80

Donner Summit 7,240 ft.

Summit Lake

Summit Lake Trail

To Hole-in-the-Ground (proposed)

Views of Castle Peak follow you up the switchbacks

3.9 Veer to the left at the fork.

4.6 Veer left up the embankment and onto the singletrack DLRT.

5.7 Merge onto the dirt road.

5.8 Turn right onto the singletrack.

6.0 Complete the first out-and-back. Veer left and begin the climb up to Donner Ridge. Expect eight switchbacks along the way.

7.3 Arrive on the ridge and an intersection with the Tahoe Donner trail system. Turn left to reach The Hut.

7.4 Arrive at The Hut for an out-of-the-wind panoramic view. Turn around and enjoy the downhill cruise.

8.8 Turn left at the fork, leaving the Donner Lake Rim Trail, and head down the access trail.

9.7 Reach the parking lot—and promise to make a contribution to Donner Lake Rim Trail effort.

34 Hole-in-the-Ground Loop

Hole-in-the-Ground is one of the premier rides in Tahoe. Well-designed and technical singletrack takes you up ridge tops to sweeping views of Castle Peak and beyond. Miles of smooth, hard-packed trails are laced with loose volcanic rubble, granite slabs, stream crossings, and more rocks. Side trips to pristine alpine lakes offer breaks along the way—and a chance to swim in the right weather.

The snow lingers up here, hiding the trail and making things soggy when it melts. It's best to let things dry out before tackling this ride. The stream crossing at Mile 12.3 can be dicey, so don't jump the gun on this ride until late July. An out-and-back to Lola Montez Lakes is a great option to maximize the singletrack and skip the tedious fire roads at the end of the loop. Either way, bring some extra tubes for all the rocks.

Start: From the Donner Summit trailhead to the Pacific Crest Trail

Distance: 16.8-mile loop

Approximate riding time: 3 to 4 hours

Difficulty rating: Intermediate to advanced—technical and moderately strenuous

Trail surface: 58 percent singletrack, 24 percent dirt road, and 18 percent paved road

Seasons: August through October

Other trail users: Hikers, equestrians, and vehicles

Land status: Tahoe National Forest

Nearest town: Soda Springs, California

Fees and permits: No fees or permits required

Schedule: 24 hours a day

Maps: Maptech CD: California, High Sierra/Tahoe; USGS maps: Soda Springs, CA; Webber Peak, CA; Norden, CA

Trail contact: Tahoe National Forest, USDA Forest Service, Truckee Ranger District, 9646 Donner Pass Road, Truckee, CA 96161; (530) 587-3558; www.fs.fed.us/r5/tahoe

Finding the trailhead: From Sacramento, drive east on U.S. Highway 80. Just before Donner Pass, take the Castle Peak-Boreal Ridge exit. Turn right at the end of the off-ramp and then left at the next road, following signs to the Pacific Crest Trail. Park in the lot at the end of the road. There is water and an outhouse here.

From Truckee, drive west on US 80 and exit on Castle Peak–Boreal Ridge. Turn left under the freeway and left again to the parking area and trailhead for the Pacific Crest Trail. **Trailhead GPS:** N 39 20.39, W 120 20.63

Miles and Directions

0.0 **START** from the entrance to the parking lot, returning down the paved road toward the freeway off-ramp.

0.3 Turn right, ride under the freeway, and turn right again onto Castle Peak Road.

0.6 Ride past the green gate onto the dirt road.

0.7 Veer right at the fork.

Zen on the Hole-in-the-Ground Trail

0.9 Veer left where a road takes off through the meadow on the right.

1.2 Stay left at the fork.

1.6 Arrive at the Hole-in-the-Ground trailhead. The well-built singletrack begins with a gradual climb through the forest and some steeply pitched switchbacks.

2.4 Climb out of the forest and onto the ridge, with sweeping views of Castle Peak to the east.

2.9 Pass a side trail to Andesite Peak on the left, and arrive at the last outlook before descending into a high-elevation basin. (**FYI:** Andesite is the loose volcanic rock you've been riding through.)

4.0 Maneuver through the rocks, and be ready to cross Lower Castle Creek in 0.5 mile.

4.8 Veer left at the trail junction, continuing toward Sand Ridge Lake.

5.4 Cross the creek on the granite slab.

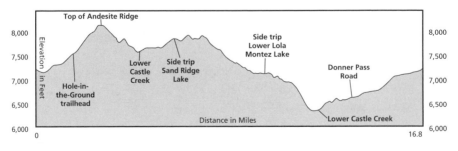

Hole-in-the-Ground Loop

RF 1 : 65,200

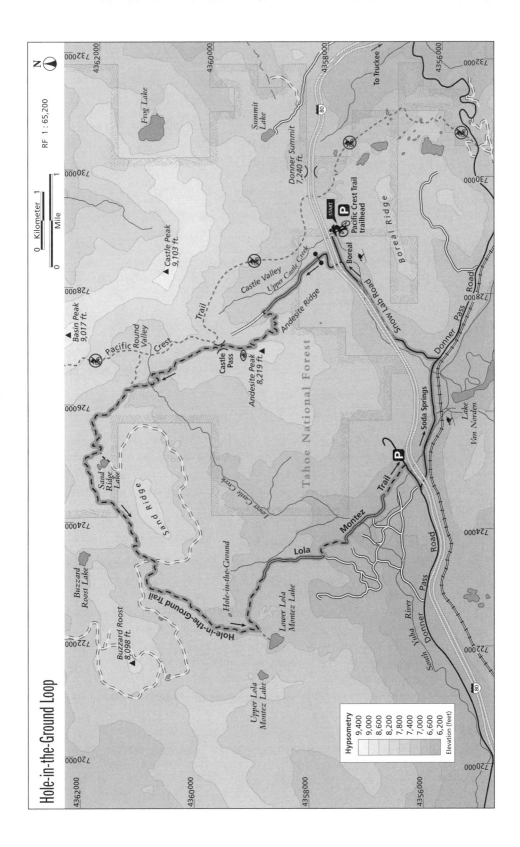

Dropping down from Andesite Ridge

5.9 Continue straight ahead at the trail junction to Sand Ridge Lake. This is an easy miss; you may blow by this without noticing. (**Side trip:** Turn left and ride 0.3 mile to this small alpine lake for a swim and a snack.)

7.1 Cross an ATV trail and continue on the singletrack. Enjoy the smooth trail while it lasts.

8.0 Go across the dirt road, and continue downhill.

9.1 Ride over slick rocks—nice.

9.8 Heads up for a steep drop at this stream crossing.

10.1 Veer left at the signed junction to lovely Lower Lola Montez Lake. Traffic on the trail may pick up now. (**Side trip:** Turn right for a short jaunt to the lake. For a great out-and-back, this is the place to turn around.)

10.5 The singletrack quickly fades into a dirt road—watch for traffic. Stay on the main downhill road for nearly a mile, ignoring all the side roads and private driveways.

11.5 Just beyond the TRAIL JUNCTION AHEAD signs, turn left to LOLA MONTEZ TRAIL TRAILHEAD. Get ready for a series of steep steps on this loose and well-worn trail.

12.0 Turn left onto the gravel road.

12.3 Ride through Lower Castle Creek, and continue on the main road, ignoring all side roads along the way.

12.9 Turn left at the TRAIL sign.

13.2 Reach the end of the singletrack at the trailhead for the Lola Montez Trail. Turn right and head down the paved frontage road.

13.5 Turn left at Donner Pass Road, cross over US 80, and follow the road through Soda Springs. There's a general store along the way to refuel if needed.

14.9 Turn left onto the dirt road at the CENTRAL SIERRA SNOW LABORATORY sign. The sign is hidden behind some pines; the road is just before a more obvious large red shed.

15.0 The road veers right and then forks. Veer left and uphill at the fork, past the PRIVATE PROPERTY sign. This is the cue to stay on the main road. Steer your course parallel to the freeway, ignoring all side roads and driveways.

16.1 Ride through the parking lot for Boreal Mountain Resort to complete the loop. Backtrack along the frontage road to the Pacific Crest Trail parking lot.

16.8 Arrive back at the start.

35 Verdi Peak Out-and-Back

Some cyclists are driven to scale high peaks. This ride is for them. The view is stunning; that's why there's an old lookout at the top and a service road to it. You can start at Boca Reservoir (5,600 feet) or drive as far as your rig or temperament takes you. The ride is a steady climb that gets rocky and a bit technical in the last 3.0 miles. There is no shame in being dropped off at the top; there just won't be the glory. From the 8,444-foot peak you can see Reno, Mount Rose, and the Granite Chief Wilderness. By summer the road gets dusty from the vehicle traffic and can be wicked hot. While you pass through cool stands of pine forest, there are plenty of open areas that heat up. Never mind that people drive this, they won't truly have touched the mountain.

Start: From Forest Service Route 72, across from Boca Rest Campground
Distance: 21.8-mile out-and-back
Approximate riding time: 4 to 5 hours
Difficulty rating: Difficult—long, strenuous climb with rocky sections near the peak
Trail surface: Wide dirt road
Seasons: May through October
Other trail users: Vehicles
Land status: Tahoe National Forest

Nearest town: Truckee, California
Fees and permits: No fees or permits required
Schedule: 24 hours a day
Maps: Maptech: California, High Sierra/Tahoe; USGS map: Boca, CA; Lake Tahoe Trail Map, Adventure Maps, Inc., 2005
Trail contact: Tahoe National Forest, USDA Forest Service, Truckee Ranger District, 9646 Donner Pass Road, Truckee, CA 96161; (530) 587-3558; www.fs.fed.us/r5/tahoe

Finding the trailhead: From Truckee, drive east on U.S. Highway 80 to the Hirschdale exit. Turn left under the freeway and continue along the eastern side of Boca Reservoir on Stampede Meadows Road. Just before Boca Rest Campground and 3.3 miles from the freeway, turn right onto FSR 72. The parking pullout immediately on the left is the trailhead for this ride. There is an outhouse back at the campground but no water. **Trailhead GPS:** N 39 25.13, W 120 05.10

Descending Verdi Peak

Miles and Directions

0.0 **START** from the pullout near the beginning of FSR 72. You will stay on this main road for the next 7.8 miles.

0.1 Ignore side road 72-01. In fact, ignore all unsigned spur and secondary roads such as 72-01, 72-04, 72-06, and so on. If the side road and main road are unsigned, follow the wider main route.

0.6 Turn right and ride past the gate, following the sign to Verde Peak. (Never mind the sign; it's *not* 13 MILES.) (**FYI:** Continue straight to reach Boca Springs Campground.)

5.3 Skip 72-24 on the right. The downhill section ahead is a nice break—but it is elevation to be gained later.

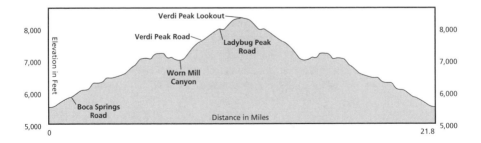

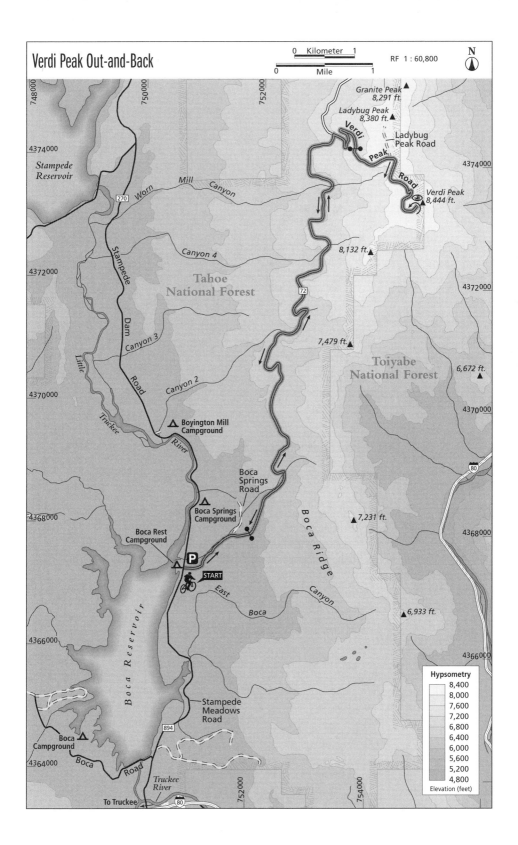

Verdi Peak Out-and-Back

RF 1 : 60,800

0 Kilometer 1

0 Mile 1

N

Granite Peak
8,291 ft.

Ladybug Peak
8,380 ft.

Verdi

Ladybug
Peak Road

Peak

Road

Verdi Peak
8,444 ft.

Stampede
Reservoir

Worn

Mill Canyon

270

8,132 ft.

4374000

4374000

Canyon 4

Tahoe
National Forest

Stampede

72

4372000

4372000

Dam

Canyon 3

7,479 ft.

Toiyabe
National Forest

6,672 ft.

Little

Road

Canyon 2

4370000

4370000

Truckee

Boyington Mill
Campground

River

80

Boca
Springs
Road

7,231 ft.

Boca Springs
Campground

B
o
c
a

R
i
d
g
e

4368000

4368000

Boca Rest
Campground

P

START

4366000

4366000

Boca

East

Canyon

Boca

R
e
s
e
r
v
o
i
r

6,933 ft.

Stampede
Meadows
Road

894

Boca
Campground

4364000

Boca

Road

Truckee
River

To Truckee   80

Hypsometry

Elevation (feet)
8,400
8,000
7,600
7,200
6,800
6,400
6,000
5,600
5,200
4,800

Elevation (feet)

748000 750000 752000 752500 754000

Snowcapped Sierra from Verdi Peak

7.8 Turn right, following the VERDE PEAK—3 MILES sign. This sign is correct. You are now leaving FSR 72.

8.9 Pass through a gate and continue straight. Ignore the impressive four-wheel shortcut on the right.

9.8 At the fork, continue straight on the DESIGNATED ROUTE. (**Side trip:** Turn left for a 0.4-mile ride to Ladybug Peak and a view of Stampede Reservoir below.)

10.9 Arrive at the end of the road, and ride the last 70 yards to the bottom of the stairs. Cleats are slippery on the metal steps, so hang on for the climb to the lookout. When you've seen it all, backtrack home.

14.0 Turn left back on FSR 72.

21.2 Turn left at the gravel road.

21.8 Arrive back at the start. The lake will feel good on a hot day.

Appendix A: Resources

California State Parks
P.O. Box 266
Tahoma, CA 96142
(530) 525–7232
www.parks.ca.gov

California Tahoe Conservancy
1061 Third Street
South Lake Tahoe, CA 96150
(530) 542–5580
www.tahoecons.ca.gov

Lake Tahoe–Nevada State Park
P.O. Box 8867
Incline Village, NV 89450
(775) 831–0494
www.parks.nv.gov

Tahoe Rim Trail Association
948 Incline Way
Incline Village, NV 89451
(775) 298–0012
www.tahoerimtrail.org
Note: Tahoe Rim Trail segment maps
are usually available at each trailhead
kiosk or can be printed directly from
www.tahoerimtrail.org.

Truckee Donner Land Trust
P.O. Box 8816
Truckee, CA 96162
(530) 583–4711
www.tdlandtrust.org

USDA Forest Service
Humboldt-Toiyabe National Forest
1536 South Carson Street
Carson City, NV 89701
(775) 882–2766
www.fs.fed.us/htnf

USDA Forest Service
Lake Tahoe Basin Management Unit
35 College Drive
South Lake Tahoe, CA 96150
(530) 543–2600
www.fs.fed.us/r5/ltbmu

USDA Forest Service
Tahoe National Forest
Truckee Ranger District
9646 Donner Pass Road
Truckee, CA 96161
(530) 587–3558
www.fs.fed.us/r5/tahoe

Trail Advocates and Clubs
Alta Alpina Cycling Club
P.O. Box 2032
Minden, NV 89423
www.altaalpinacyclingclub.com

The Reno Wheelmen
P.O. Box 12832
Reno, NV 89510-2832
www.renowheelmen.org

Tahoe Area Mountain Bicycling
Association
www.tambaonline.com

Additional References
Hauserman, Tim. *The Tahoe Rim Trail,*
Wilderness Press, Berkeley, CA, 2002

Lake Tahoe Trail Map, Adventure Maps,
Inc., 2005; www.adventuremaps.net

Appendix B: Mountain Bike Parks

Northstar at Tahoe
California Highway 276 and Northstar Drive
P.O. Box 129
Truckee, CA 96160
(800) 466–6784 or (530) 562–2268
www.skinorthstar.com

Kirkwood
California Highway 88 between Silver Lake and Caples Lake
1501 Kirkwood Meadows Drive
Kirkwood, CA 95646
(209) 258–6000
www.kirkwood.com

Appendix C: Paved Bike Paths

In addition to an increasing number of designated bike lanes appearing along the roads in the Tahoe area, there are some wonderful paved bike paths. These trails have gentle grades and are popular spots for families, strollers, and joggers. They also offer access and links to many of the rides in this book.

Tahoe City

These paths are easily accessible from the Truckee River access parking area on the west side of California Highway 89, just south of the junction with California Highway 28.

Truckee River Recreation Trail. Runs 4.5 miles along the Truckee River from Tahoe City to the entrance to Squaw Valley. A bike lane along CA 89 continues to Truckee.

Squaw Valley. Runs 2.0 miles up Squaw Valley Road to Squaw Valley U.S.A. Starts at CA 89, near the end of the Truckee River Recreation Trail.

West Lake Bike Path. Runs about 10.0 miles along CA 89 from Tahoe City to Sugar Pine Point State Park. While most of the pathway is a discrete trail, it crosses the highway several times. At times it turns into a bike lane on the shoulder of CA 89 or runs on side streets along the way.

Dollar Point Trail. Runs nearly 2.3 miles along CA 28 from the State Recreation Area Campground on the eastern side of Tahoe City to the Dollar Point neighborhood.

Tahoe Vista

North Lake Tahoe Regional Park Bike Path. Runs 1.2 miles from the soccer field, through the forest, to Pinedrop Street near California Highway 267.

Incline Village

Lakeshore Boulevard Bike Path. Runs approximately 3 miles along Lakeshore Boulevard between Nevada Highway 28 on each end.

South Shore

South Lake Bike Path. Runs 6.5 miles between downtown South Lake Tahoe (the junction of Pioneer Trail and Lake Tahoe Boulevard) and the Y junction of CA 89 and U.S. Highway 50. Bike route signs mark the way as this route weaves through the city. The pathway morphs from newly paved path to residential streets, and in places it's either a busy shoulder or a sidewalk.

Pope Valley–Baldwin Bike Path. Runs nearly 4 miles along CA 89. It starts from the outdoor bicycle rental just north of the Y, to Spring Creek Road just beyond Baldwin Beach.

Appendix D: Campgrounds

Most campgrounds in the Tahoe area are open late May (Memorial Day weekend) through October. Having said that, it's best to check before you travel, since each campground is slightly different. The usual caveat remains: It all depends on the snowfall. Reservations are your safest bet; the popular campgrounds on the lake fill up fast.

North Lake Area

Lake Forest Campground, Tahoe City Public Utility District, 1.5 miles east of Tahoe City on Lake Forest Road; (530) 583–3796; www.tahoecitypud.com/parks rec/fields.shtml#2

Mount Rose, Toiyabe National Forest, 7.8 miles north of Incline Village on Nevada Highway 431; (775) 882–2766; reservations: (877) 444–6777; www.reserveusa.com

Sandy Beach, near Kings Beach, 6873 North Lake Boulevard, Tahoe Vista; (530) 546–7682

Silver Creek, 8 miles south of Truckee on California Highway 89; (530) 587–3558; reservations: (877) 444–6777; www.reserveusa.com

Tahoe State Recreation Area (SRA), east side of Tahoe City on California Highway 28; (530) 583–3074; www.parks.ca.gov; (800) 444–7275; www.reserveamerica.com

South Lake Area

Bayview Campground, 7.7 miles north of South Lake Tahoe on CA 89; (530) 543–2600; www.forestcamping.com/dow/pacficsw/ltbcmp.htm

Campground by the Lake, City of South Lake Tahoe, 1150 Rufus Allen Boulevard off U.S. Highway 50, South Lake Tahoe; (530) 542–6096; www.recreationintahoe .com/campground.htm.

Camp Richardson Resort & Marina, 1900 Jameson Beach Road, 2.5 miles north of South Lake Tahoe on CA 89; (530) 541–1801; reservations: (800) 544–1801; www.camprich.com

Emerald Bay State Park, 6.5 miles north of South Lake Tahoe on CA 89; (530) 541–3030; www.parks.ca.gov; reservations: (800) 444–7275; www.reserveamerica.com

Fallen Leaf Campground, 2165 Fallen Leaf Road, 3 miles north of South Lake Tahoe off CA 89; (530) 544–0426; www.fs.fed.us/r5/ltbmu/recreation/camping/ flcamp.shtml; reservations: (877) 444–6777; www.reserveusa.com

**KOA Kampground, 760 US 50, South Lake Tahoe; (530) 577–3693; reservations: (800) KOA–3477; www.koa.com/where/ca/05148/index.htm

Nevada Beach, Elk Point Road off US 50, Zephyr Cove; (775) 588–5562; www.fs.fed.us/r5/ltbmu/recreation/camping/nvbeach.shtml; reservations: (877) 444–6777; www.reserveusa.com

Tahoe Pines Campground, 860 US 50, South Lake Tahoe; (530) 577–1653; www.tahoepinescampground.com

**Tahoe Valley Campground, 1175 Melba Drive, just south of the Y on US 50 in South Lake Tahoe; (530) 541–2222, (877) 717–8737; www.rvonthego.com

**Zephyr Cove Resort, 760 US 50, Zephyr Cove; (775) 588–6644; reservations: (775) 589–4981

West Lake Area

D. L. Bliss State Park, 10.5 miles north of South Lake Tahoe on CA 89; (530) 525–7277; www.parks.ca.gov; reservations: (800) 444–7275; www.reserveamerica.com

Kaspian Bicycle Campground, 4 miles south of Tahoe City on CA 89; access by bike or foot only; (530) 544–5994; www.fs.fed.us/r5/ltbmu/recreation/camping/kaspian.shtml; reservations: (877) 444-6777; www.reserveusa.com

Meeks Bay, 11 miles south of Tahoe City on CA 89; (530) 544–5994; www.fs.fed.us/r5/ltbmu/recreation/camping/meeks.shtml; reservations: (877) 444–6777; www.reserveusa.com

Meeks Bay Resort & Marina, 7941 Emerald Bay Road, Meeks Bay, 10.6 miles south of Tahoe City on CA 89; (530) 525–6946; www.meeksbayresort.com; reservations: (877) 444–6777; www.reserveusa.com

**Sugar Pine Point State Park, 9 miles south of Tahoe City on CA 89; (530) 525–7982; www.parks.ca.gov; reservations: (800) 444–7275; www.reserveamerica.com

William Kent Campground, 2 miles south of Tahoe City on CA 89; (530) 583–3642; www.fs.fed.us/r5/ltbmu/; reservations: (877) 444–6777; www.reserveusa.com

Truckee Area

Alder Creek Campground, 13813 Alder Creek Road, Tahoe Donner; (530) 587–9462; www.tahoedonner.com

Boca Campground, on west shore of Boca Reservoir, 7 miles east of Truckee; exit US 80 at Hirschdale; (530) 587–3558

Boca Rest Campground, on Boca Reservoir, 9.5 miles east of Truckee; exit US 80 at Hirschdale; (530) 587–3558

Boca Springs Campground, 2 miles east of Boca Reservoir, on Boca Springs Road; exit US 80 at Hirschdale; (530) 587–3558

Boyington Mill Campground, on Boca-Stampede Road, between Boca and Stampede Reservoirs, 10 miles northeast of Truckee; exit US 80 at Hirschdale; (530) 587–3558; reservations: (877) 444–6777; www.reserveusa.com

Donner Memorial State Park, on Donner Lake; (530) 582–7892; www.parks .ca.gov; reservations: (800) 444–7275; www.reserveamerica.com

Goose Meadows Campground, 6 miles south of Truckee on CA 89; (530) 587–3558; reservations: (877) 444–6777; www.reserveusa.com

Granite Flat Campground, 2 miles south of Truckee on CA 89; (530) 587–3558; reservations: (877) 444–6777; www.reserveusa.com

Logger Camp, south side of Stampede Reservoir, 15 miles northeast of Truckee; exit US 80 at Hirschdale; (530) 587–3558; reservations: (877) 444–6777; www.reserveusa.com

Martis Creek Lake, 1 mile south of Truckee Airport, off CA 267; (530) 639–2342

Prosser Creek Reservoir, 2 miles north of Truckee on Prosser Recreation Access Road, off CA 89; (530) 587–3558

★★Open year-round

Appendix E: Lodges

The Sierra Club's Clair Tappaan Lodge
19550 Donner Pass Road
P.O. Box 36
Norden, CA 95724
(530) 426–3632 or (800) 679–6775
www.sierraclub.org/outings/lodges/ctl/

Cal Lodge
P.O. Box 63
Norden, CA 95724
(530) 426–3341
www.cal-lodge.com

Index

Angora Lakes Out-and-Back 107

Antone Meadows Loop 37

Armstrong Pass to Saxon Creek Loop 85

Big Meadow to Pacific Crest Trail
Out-and-Back 88

Blackwood Canyon to Ellis Lake
Out-and-Back 15

Brockway Summit to Mount Baldy
Out-and-Back 47

Brockway Summit to Tahoe City
Point-to-Point 42

Burnside Lake Out-and-Back 91

Cold Creek Loop 79

Corral Trail Loop 82

Donner Lake Rim Trail Out-and-Back
125

Emigrant Trail to Alder Creek
Out-and-Back 122

Emigrant Trail to Stampede Reservoir
Out-and-Back 118

Fallen Leaf Lake Loop 109

Flume Trail Loop 60

General Creek Loop with
Out-and-Back to Lost Lake 12

Gun Mount Loop 100

Hawley Grade Point-to-Point 93

Hole-in-the-Ground Loop 129

Kingsbury Grade to Big Meadow
Point-to-Point 71

Kingsbury Grade to South Camp Peak
Out-and-Back 67

Lower Blackwood Canyon Loop 19

North Lake Tahoe Regional Park 40

North Tahoe City Loop 33

Page Meadows Double Loop 25

Power Line Loop 74

Sawtooth Ridge Trail Loop 114

Scott Peak Loop 30

Spooner Summit to South Camp Peak
Out-and-Back 64

Stanford Rock Loop 22

Tahoe Meadows to Marlette Lake to
Flume Trail Point-to-Point 54

Tyrolean Point-to-Point 51

Upper Truckee River Out-and-Back
104

Verdi Peak Out-and-Back 133

Washoe Meadows Out-and-Back 96

About the Author

Undergraduate and graduate school at the University of California at Davis and Berkeley brought Lorene Jackson to northern California, and she never left. Gradually moving up the ranks of cross-country racing, she has won the expert division of her age group at the NORBA national races. More recently, she can be found racing mountain bike triathlons and working with Trips for Kids, a national nonprofit that takes disadvantaged youth on mountain bike adventures (www.tripsforkids.org). This trail guide has been an excuse to lift her head up from the training rides, explore the high country, and smell the wildflowers. Lorene is a native Californian, mother of three sons, and the author of *Mountain Biking the San Francisco Bay Area* (FalconGuide, 2003).